Soul Food Cookbook for Two

365-Day Perfectly Portioned Recipes
with Favorite Southern Comfort Food for Healthy Eating

Syen Nost

Table of Contents

Introduction

No one eats quite like Southerners, and the uniqueness of this American cuisine goes far beyond fried chicken, black-eyed peas, and greens. Southerners do everything a little differently, including breakfast. If you just need to make meals for two, this book will be your best choice.

Ditch the refined and processed ingredients and reawaken your taste buds to the vibrant flavors of soul foods that will satisfy your hunger and leave you feeling happier. Soul Food Cookbook for Two makes it easy with different recipes for with Favorite Southern Comfort Food for Healthy Eating. This essential couple's cookbook has more than just tasty and wholesome recipes inside.

The soul cook is popular to all. But getting started can feel like an overwhelming lifestyle change—especially if you're doing it alone. Soul Food Cookbook for Two is here to help by teaching you how to embrace the soul food with two people in mind.

Chapter 2: Basics ofSoul Food

What Is Soul Food?

Soul food was created by the West African people who were stolen and brought as enslaved people to America. The term "soul food" was not actually created until the 1960s during the civil rights movement. It was born of a strong sense of pride within the black community. Even though the term was coined only somewhat recently, the cuisine has been around for a long time.

Soul food flavors and dishes are versatile, partly because of the movement of enslaved people who often were moved around throughout the South, from the Carolinas to Alabama to Tennessee. Creole and Gullah cuisines are examples of soul food variations that developed with the movement of enslaved people who used whatever native ingredients were readily available to create flavorful, soulful food to feed themselves and their families. The resiliency of enslaved people was shown by their ability to use unwanted scraps such as pig intestines, ears, and feet to create flavorful, hearty meals. As enslaved people were moved from place to place, soul food cuisine expanded. Enslaved people merged their own food knowledge with French and European influences, resulting in many now-classic dishes such as gumbo, jambalaya, and chowder.

Over the years, soul food and other southern styles of cooking were deemed unhealthy. Soul food was known as a poor man's diet. The popularity of heavily fried, highly processed, and sugar-loaded foods, along with a lack of access to fresh vegetables and fruits, has contributed to a rise in illnesses like heart disease, hypertension, and diabetes within the African American community. According to the Centers for Disease Control and Prevention (CDC), African Americans ages 18 to 49 are twice as likely to die from heart disease as whites, and African Americans ages 35 to 64 are 50 percent more likely to have high blood pressure. The recipes I've created in this book prove that soul food doesn't have to be loaded with meat and dairy or be deep-fried or sugar-coated to be comforting and delicious. After trying these recipes, you'll feel happier, more energized, and on the road to a healthier you.

I use two definitions of soul food to guide my work and my own eating. The first is the acronym SOUL: Seasonal, Organic, Unprocessed, Local. Eating foods that are seasonally grown, organic, when possible, unprocessed, or whole, and grown locally will go a long way toward helping you become the healthiest version of yourself. The standard American diet (SAD) tends to be high in processed convenience foods and is often high in unhealthy fats, sugars, and chemical additives. Eating the SAD way has proven to be detrimental to our health, our planet, and the lives of millions of innocent animals, so I say, let's eat the SOUL way.

My second definition of soul food is more of an energy or feeling that should be a central part of making soul food. Soul food has to be made with the love and energy of the soul poured into each dish. Soul food can't be created by just anyone. You must put love, passion, and joy into every step to make the food truly soulful. Soul food is pure love on a plate!

Veganizing Soul Food

Soul food gets a bad rap because it's typically filled with unhealthy ingredients like butter, sugar, and meat and can use unhealthy preparations like deep-frying. In this cookbook, you'll discover that most of the recipes consist of whole-food, plant-based ingredients that are fairly easy to find. Most vegans I know didn't become vegan because they woke up one day and decided they didn't like the taste of meat or dairy. Most chose this lifestyle for health reasons and because of the senseless murder of millions of animals on a daily basis. All that death just so we can eat! Creating vegan soul food was important for me to prove to myself that I could still have all my favorite comfort foods without harming any animals. By creating compassionate food, we not only save lives, but we also greatly decrease our carbon footprint and help save the planet as well.

Veganizing soul food has been such a fun and tasty process. Being able to research and play around with so many exciting and new (to me) plant-based ingredients has opened a new door of creativity in the kitchen. The vegan lifestyle has recently gained popularity, as evidenced by the huge rise in vegan products that are readily available at most supermarkets. For some people, buying mock meats and other prepared vegan foods can help with the transition to a vegan lifestyle. However, many of these foods are highly processed and not necessarily healthy. If you're transitioning into veganism or just looking to eat healthier, I recommend limiting mock meats and other prepared foods. Instead, I encourage you to visit your local farmer's market and experiment with fresh vegetables and fruits to incorporate into your new lifestyle.

The dishes and recipes compiled in this cookbook were specifically designed to pay homage to classic soul food staples while using healthier ingredients and cooking techniques and without compromising the delicious flavors of traditional soul food. One of my goals in writing this book was to show the world how healthy, delicious, and amazing vegan soul food can be. I can't guarantee that every recipe in this book is 100 percent healthy, but I can guarantee that by replacing meat and dairy with plant-based ingredients, my version is healthier than the original. For example, my Buffalo Popcorn Chickenless Bites recipe is made with tofu, which is high in protein and is a great replacement for chicken lovers.

Veganism and Health

People eat meat and think they will become strong as an ox, forgetting that the ox eats grass. —Giuseppe Caruso

"Why goes vegan?" is a question I get asked almost daily. My answer is that going vegan not only lowers your risk of developing chronic illness and disease, but it also helps reduce our carbon footprint and save the lives of animals. I initially chose to go vegan to see whether it would help cure my hypertension and borderline type 2 diabetes. Much to my surprise, within my first 30 days of going vegan, my blood sugar levels, and blood pressure levels normalized, and I no longer had to take prescription medication daily. I was amazed! Many studies have shown that heavy consumption of meat and dairy products is directly linked to chronic illnesses including cancer, hypertension, heart disease, type 2 diabetes, and more. A recent study initiated by the American Heart Association concluded that following a vegan diet for five weeks may decrease risk factors for heart disease, the leading killer of all Americans.

In African American communities today, it is common to have one or more family members or close friends who have been diagnosed with type 2 diabetes, cancer, or hypertension. Why are these diseases so common in our communities over others? The common link seems to be diet. Food is a big part of African American culture and community, but unfortunately, many of us have learned unhealthy ways of cooking that have been passed down from generation to generation. According to U.S. News & World Report, a recent study in JAMA concluded that the high-fat, high-sugar, high-sodium traditional southern diet leads to hypertension and heart disease and may be linked to high incidences of these illnesses in the African American community. I think it's time we try a new and better lifestyle that will contribute to extending our lives and strengthening our communities by giving our bodies the pure and natural foods they desire.

Vegan diets can also help protect against certain cancers and stabilize blood sugars, reducing the risk of developing diabetes. I personally was greatly influenced by the documentary What the Health. This movie really helped me understand the damage that consuming animal products inflicts on our bodies.

Since we are talking about veganism and health, I think it's important to include the health of our planet. Animal agriculture is the single largest contributor of harmful emissions and is breaking down the ozone layers in the atmosphere. In order to raise animals for mass consumption, we have cut down massive sections of the rain forest, and this has greatly contributed to wildlife extinction. Our false belief that we need to feed ourselves using animals is literally killing not only us but millions of innocent beings and the planet we all share.

If you want to live longer and be healthier, start by eating more plant-based foods. We can make a difference in our health and our world, starting with our food choices. Let's eat to live!

Healthy Vegan Guidelines

These practical tips will help you maintain a healthy vegan lifestyle.

- **Read Labels.**
Avoiding animal products is crucial when transitioning. You'll be surprised how many of your favorite foods have some form of animal product in them. Some animal by-products have names that may not be familiar at first, like whey, whey powder, casein, lactose, and gelatin. I always read the ingredients, and sometimes the bottom of the ingredient list will say whether there are milk or dairy products included. All necessary protein and nutrients needed for the body can be found in plant forms. Animals get their protein from plants, so just bypass the middleman and get all your vitamins, nutrients, and protein directly from the source.

- **Eat the Rainbow.**
Not only will eating vegetables of all different colors help make your dishes vibrant and beautiful, but each color fruit or vegetable has phytonutrients that basically are the nutrients of that fruit or vegetable. Red fruits and vegetables like tomatoes, red peppers, and strawberries have vitamins A and C, antioxidants, and manganese. Green vegetables and fruits like broccoli, cabbage, cucumbers, and kale contain vitamins B and K, folate, and potassium. Orange vegetables and fruits like carrots, oranges, sweet potatoes, and cantaloupe contain vitamins C, A, and B6, as well as antioxidants. Purple vegetables and fruits like eggplant, red onions, purple potatoes, plums, and blueberries contain B vitamins and antioxidants. White produce such as cauliflower, garlic, mushrooms, and potatoes contain vitamins K and C. If you eat a variety of colors on your plate each week, you are more likely to get the vitamins and nutrients your body needs.

- **Follow the 80/20 Rule.**

You'll hear this frequently in health-conscious communities. I love this rule primarily because it allows you to eat healthy 80 percent of the time and indulge in small amounts of fried or processed foods and desserts the other 20 percent of the time. This gives you a great balance, and you really don't feel like you're missing anything.

- **Turn Up the Flavor.**

One of the most important things in going vegan is to have a happy palate. Adding fresh herbs and using a creative variety of seasoning blends will go a long way toward making your mouth smile. Embrace the vegan wholefood, plant-based lifestyle by getting creative with vegetables and fruits. You'll consume everything your body needs through plants, legumes, nuts, fruits, and grains.

How to Cook from This Book

On this cooking journey we are about to embark on, you can expect to learn easy and creative techniques to transform traditional soul food favorites into healthier versions. We'll discuss some history and origins of southern staples and explore how and what is needed to veganize these dishes. Then we will explore the health benefits and nutritional value of staple vegan ingredients and how they are used. Next is the fun part. We get to play with food! I have shared 101 plant-based vegan soul food recipes in this book for you to experiment with and enjoy.

All recipes include labels like gluten-free, oil-free, nut-free, or soy-free. Dishes that can be prepared in 30 minutes or less are labeled, too. In the following pages, you will find some key general information to set you up for success on this vegan soul food journey. Happy cooking!

Improvise

The wonderful thing about creating in the kitchen is the ability to improvise. This is one reason cooking tops baking for me. Baking has to be precise, but with cooking you can add additional ingredients if you feel like your recipe is missing something. I'd highly suggest that you try all the recipes as instructed once; then when you have a good idea of the taste and flavor profile you're looking for, feel free to play around with different ingredients to create your own take. For example, the Caribbean Coconut Greens recipe can be made with less coconut cream if you're not a big fan of coconut flavor, or you can increase the amount of liquid smoke to give it a stronger smoky taste. It really just depends on what your palate likes and how creative you'd like to get. With most recipes, some ingredients can be switched out depending on what ingredients you might already have on hand. Soul food is the perfect food to get creative with. Infuse it with love and make it your own.

Southern Staples

There are certain staple ingredients that go along with any regional cuisine. In this section, I list and describe some of the key staples that will be used in the recipes that follow.

Vegetables

Corn or maize dates back at least 6,000 years and evolved from teosinte, which is a wild grass. Corn was developed by ancient Mexicans, adopted by Native Americans, and easily accessible to enslaved people because it was cheap and easy to grow. Corn is rich in vitamin B1 and vitamin C and has a good amount of fiber. Since corn production in the United States has greatly increased over the past century, it is now mass-produced, and I recommend purchasing organic, non-GMO (genetically modified organism) corn if possible.

Collards are the oldest members of the cabbage family and were grown by the ancient Greeks. Collards are a good source of protein and fiber and also contain folic acid, vitamin A, vitamin C, calcium, potassium, iron, and zinc. Collards were known as a poor man's food during slavery and remain inexpensive. They are usually cooked with other greens like mustard, turnip, dandelion, or kale. Collards have large leaves, are slightly bitter, and can be on the tougher side.

Kale is considered a superfood because of its amazing nutrient density. It's high in fiber, protein, and vitamins A, C, and K and contains folate, which is great for brain development. Kale is not as tough as collard greens and is a great addition to soups, stews, salads, burgers, and smoothies.

Dandeliongreens are high in vitamins A, C, and K. This green helps the absorption of iron. It also contains essential and trace minerals. This bitter green should be used in smaller amounts in salads, so the strong taste does not overpower the dish.

Sweetpotato is a root vegetable and was a staple ingredient for African enslaved people. Sweet potatoes are sweet, starchy, and rich in vitamins, antioxidants, fiber, and minerals. Sweet potatoes can be used in many dishes, from pies to soups to casseroles.

Cabbage contains potassium, vitamin B1, fiber, folate, manganese, and vitamin B6. Fried cabbage will always be a favorite dish of mine. Find my recipe here.

Greenbeans, also known as pole beans, are high in folate, thiamin, riboflavin, iron, magnesium, and potassium. These delicious beans are thought to have originated in Central America and are now very popular in southern-style cooking.

Fruits

Watermelon grows well in the southern states and became known as a poor man's food because enslaved people were able to grow, eat, and sell it after emancipation. Watermelon is sweet, juicy, and hydrating, along with being high in vitamins C and A, antioxidants, and potassium. When in season, watermelon is my favorite fruit. Watermelon barbecue sauce, fresh watermelon juice, and adding watermelon to salads are just a few ways to use this delicious fruit.

Peaches are soft, juicy, and fragrant. They grow abundantly in all of the southern states, and, of course, Georgia is known for its amazing sweet peaches. If you love peaches, wait until you try my Peaches and Cream French Toast.

Blackberries grow abundantly across the United States. They are high in fiber, antioxidants, and vitamin K and can easily be made into syrup, cobblers, jams, or preServes:.

Plums were brought to America around the seventeenth century. They are high in fiber and natural sugar that doesn't spike blood sugar. Plums are a tasty addition to salads, are great as a snack, and can be made into sweet and savory sauces.

Beans and Legumes

Limabeans or butter beans have a sweet, smooth, and buttery flavor that has made them very popular in southern-style cooking. These beans pair well with corn and potatoes and are a great addition to soups and stews.

Black-eyedpeas or cowpeas are one of the most well-known ingredients in soul food cuisine. These beans originated in West Africa and arrived in America sometime in the 1700s. They are traditionally cooked in an African American home during the holidays and especially at New Year's, as they are a symbol of good luck and prosperity. They are high in protein, iron, and fiber.

Kidneybeans are another staple in soul food cuisine. They show up in such common dishes as rice and beans or chili. These red beans are high in vitamins and minerals and are a great source of protein.

Lentils are one of my favorites and are the most versatile pulses for vegan cooking. Lentils are small in size but hearty in texture and flavor, making them a terrific meat replacement. This tiny bean is a nutrient powerhouse, leading the way in protein among legumes and also containing potassium, folate, iron, and fiber. Try my Peach-Habanero Barbecue Lentil Mini Loaves.

Peanuts, or groundnuts, were brought to America by enslaved people from West Africa in the 1700s. Even though "nut" is in the name, peanuts are actually legumes. Peanuts are high in fiber, protein, healthy fats, magnesium, calcium, and iron. Boiled peanuts are a southern favorite passed down from West African enslaved people.

Spices

Dried thyme is a savory pungent herb that is used a lot in Caribbean cooking. You'll see this wonderful spice in many recipes in this book. Thyme has a unique earthy flavor that blends wonderfully in soul food.

White pepper has a mild but distinct flavor. Black and white pepper are used for different flavoring purposes in soul cooking. White pepper should be used in more lightly seasoned recipes like my Plum-Tahini Dressing.

Cayenne or red pepper is spicy and is used to add a kick to many soul food, Caribbean, and Creole dishes.

Kelppowder comes from a sea vegetable that is high in potassium, magnesium, calcium, iron, and iodine. Kelp, or nori, has a sea taste and is ideal to use in recipes like my Cajun Crabless Jackfruit Balls or my Fishless Banana-Blossom Fish.

Apple cider vinegar is derived from fermented apple juice. Fermented foods have good gut bacteria in them that aid in digestion. Look for brands that are organic and that have the cloudy "mother" in them. I use this ingredient in several baking recipes as well as in dressings, marinades, and sauces. Apple cider vinegar improves heart health, assists in stabilizing blood sugar, aids in weight loss, kills harmful gut bacteria, and lowers cholesterol.

Nutritional yeast or "nooch" is inactive yeast that can be grown on blackstrap molasses or sugar beets. It has a light, buttery, cheesy flavor and is high in protein, fiber, minerals, and vitamins. Nooch is commonly used in vegan cooking to replace the flavor of cheese. It's great on popcorn, in macaroni and cheese, in sauces, or as a topping on salads.

Bay leaves have a soft, floral, somewhat earthy tone. Bay leaves are commonly used in soups, stews, rice dishes, and cooked grains.

Onion powder has a more concentrated taste compared to onions. Fresh onions and onion powder are commonly used to maximize flavor profiles in southern vegan cooking.

Liquid smoke is one of my favorite ingredients to use in soulful cooking. It adds that full, round flavor of smokiness that is truly needed in vegan soul food. I use this spice in many dishes, like my Smoky Tempeh Bacon, and my Three-Bean Chili.

Smoked paprika can have a variety of heat levels, from mild to spicy. I usually look for a milder version because the smoky flavor stands out more in dishes. The smoky undertones in this spice are a wonderful complement in vegan soul food cooking.

Granulated garlic is a coarse grade of dried garlic that I prefer to use in most recipes, as I have found that the flavor profile is stronger than garlic powder. Garlic is a good source of iron, copper, manganese, and phosphorus.

Sweeteners

Cane sugar has long been associated with slavery, beginning in the Caribbean. Settlers first brought cane sugar to America, specifically Louisiana, around the 1700s. White sugar is cane sugar that has been refined using animal bone char to remove any impurities. This is not vegan and should be avoided. Organic cane sugar is what is usually found in my pantry.

Maple syrup is a wonderful, tasty sweetener derived from the sap of maple trees that traditionally grow in the northern states. It is a great ingredient for southern cuisine and baking and can be used in place of corn syrups, which are highly processed and mass-produced.

Brown sugar is simply cane sugar that has kept some of the natural molasses during refinement. Brown sugar is delicious in baking, sauces, and dressings.

Coconut sugar is a low-glycemic sugar made from the sap of the coconut palm. This sugar can be used as a 1:1 replacement for brown sugar in many baking recipes.

Molasses has the lowest sugar content of cane sugars. It is a thick, dark syrup that is made by boiling down cane sugar or sugar beets. This syrup is high in iron, calcium, and magnesium and is great in baking or making sauces.

Agave nectar is harvested from the core of the agave plant and usually comes from Mexico. This sweetener is a great replacement for honey and is good for diabetics because it does not spike blood sugar as much as cane sugar does.

Pantry

- **Vegetable stock cubes** are used to add flavor and seasoning to many dishes in this cookbook. These cubes can be fairly high in sodium, so beware if adding additional salt.

- **Ground flax meal** is used as a binder in many recipes in this cookbook. Mixing flax meal with water creates a thick liquid called a "flax egg," which is used in vegan baking.

- **Coconut cream** is a thicker version of coconut milk. I use this in soups, stews, and baking.

- **Almond milk** is my favorite nut milk option. I believe it to taste most like cow's milk out of all the nut milks.

- **Tamari** is a gluten-free soy sauce that can be used in place of salt in many sauces.

- **Earth Balance** is my favorite vegan butter. I've tried most of the ones out there, and this one has just the right amount of water content and Serves:baking a breeze.

- **Grapeseed oil** can be used in dressings, frying, sautéing, and baking. This is a high-heat oil and is recommended for alkaline cooking.

- **Sunflower oil** is a light oil that I like to use for dressings, sauces, frying, and baking.

- **Unbleached all-purpose flour** should be stored in a sealed container. Bob's Red Mill Gluten-Free 1-to-1 Baking Flour can be used as a replacement flour if you want to make some of the recipes in this book gluten-free.

- **Baking soda** is a leavener, which means it helps dough rise and Serves:baked goods fluffy.

- **Baking powder** is also a leavener but has a much lighter taste.

- **Cornmeal** is finely ground corn that is used in batters, corn bread, and my favorite, hush puppies.

- **Firm or extra-firm tofu** is made from soybeans and is used commonly in vegan cooking. I use it as a scrambled-egg replacement or for mock "chicken" bits. It needs to be refrigerated.

- **Panko bread crumbs** are Japanese bread crumbs that give a perfectly crunchy coating to cauliflower wings, avocado fries, and more.

- **Tempeh** is fermented tofu that is used mainly as a bacon replacement in this cookbook, but it can be used in a variety of vegan recipes.

- **Textured vegetable protein** or TVP is freeze-dried tofu granules. It is great in vegan burgers, sausage, pot pies, and more to add protein and meaty texture.

- **Applesauce** is used in this cookbook as a replacement for eggs. I use ⅓ cup applesauce per egg for a super-moist dessert.

- **Just mayo and best foods vegan mayo** are my favorites in the vegan mayo department. They are the closest to regular mayonnaise in flavor and texture and can be used just as you would nonvegan brands.

- **Grits** are made with finely ground white corn and are a staple in southern cuisine.

- **Pecans** are commonly used in soul food baking. They have a buttery taste and are mainly cultivated in Georgia, Texas, and Mexico.

- **Canned diced tomatoes** are a quick and easy way to add flavor and depth to many recipes, especially soups and stews.

- **Tomato paste** is a thick paste made by slow-cooking tomatoes with the seeds and skin strained out. This paste is great to thicken, flavor, and enhance dishes.

- **Potatoes** play a big role in soul food— for example, in recipes like Cajun Potato Salad, and Garlic-Smashed Potatoes

- **Brown basmati** rice is something I prefer over regular brown rice because it is more fragrant, takes less time to cook, and is hard to overcook.

- **Vital wheat gluten** is a protein that is extracted from wheat. It is over 80 percent protein and is used to make many commercial mock meats.

So now that we have covered what, why, and how of veganism and soul food, it's time to let the fun begin. Next, you'll find all the vegan soul food recipes you'll need to assist you on this journey to a healthier, more compassionate, more soulful you!

Chapter 3: Breakfast

Loaded Sweet Potato Hash

Looking for a hearty, filling breakfast for you and the family? Here it is! This recipe provides a good balance of starches from the vegetables and protein from the tofu. When my sons were younger and busy with athletic activities, I made this dish often. This is also a great way to use up leftover tofu scramble.

Makes 2servings

Ingredients:

- 1 medium sweet potato, peeled and shredded
- 2 medium red potatoes, shredded
- ⅓ cup diced red or yellow bell pepper
- 1 medium red onion, diced
- 3 garlic cloves, minced
- 1 teaspoon sea salt
- ½ teaspoon smoked paprika
- 1 teaspoon onion powder
- 1 teaspoon dried rosemary
- 1 teaspoon dried thyme
- 1 teaspoon dried sage
- 1 teaspoon freshly ground black pepper
- Pinch cayenne pepper (optional)
- 6 tablespoons grapeseed or sunflower oil, divided
- ½ cup stemmed, finely sliced collard greens
- ½ cup seasoned tofu (from the Farmhouse Scramble recipe)

Directions:

1. In a medium mixing bowl, combine the shredded sweet and red potatoes, bell pepper, onion, garlic, sea salt, paprika, onion powder, rosemary, thyme, sage, black pepper, cayenne pepper (if using), and 1½ tablespoons of oil and stir to mix well.
2. Heat a griddle or cast-iron skillet over medium-high heat and add 3 tablespoons of oil. Once the oil is hot, spoon the potato mixture using a medium ice cream scoop (about 2.75 ounces) onto the griddle and flatten slightly.
3. Cook for 5 to 7 minutes or until desired crispiness. When the potato mounds are slightly crispy and turning golden brown, turn them over and move them closer together to create space on the griddle.

4. In the space on the griddle, drizzle the remaining 1½ tablespoons of oil, add the collards and tofu scramble, and sauté for 3 to 4 minutes.
5. Remove the hash mounds to a plate and top with the scramble, and collards.

Peaches and Cream French Toast

When you start your morning off with a delicious, filling breakfast, you feel like you can conquer the world. I created this recipe some years ago when my children were still small. Saturday mornings in my house included a smorgasbord of breakfast dishes for my boys. This dish was always the first to disappear. When peaches are in season, try white peaches for an even sweeter dish.

Makes 2 servings

Ingredients:

For The Whipped Cream

- 1 (15-ounce) can coconut whipping cream, kept in refrigerator overnight
- 2 tablespoons maple syrup

Directions:

1. Remove the can of coconut cream from the refrigerator. Chilling the cream thickens the liquid, which helps the whipping process.
2. Place the cream in a deep mixing bowl and add the maple syrup.
3. Using a handheld mixer, whip on maximum speed for 3 to 4 minutes, until the cream is thick and forms peaks.
4. Put the bowl back into the refrigerator until the other recipe components are done.

For The Sauce

- 2 or 3 fresh peaches, washed and sliced, or 8 ounces frozen peaches, thawed
- ⅓ teaspoon cinnamon
- ½ teaspoon vanilla
- 1 tablespoon brown sugar
- ½ tablespoon cane sugar
- 1 tablespoon Earth Balance vegan butter

Directions:

1. In a medium mixing bowl, stir together the peaches, cinnamon, vanilla, brown sugar, and cane sugar and set aside.

2. Melt the butter in a medium saucepan over medium heat; then add the peach mixture and stir. Cover and allow to cook for 6 to 8 minutes or until the peaches are tender and a caramel sauce has developed and thickened.
3. Turn off the heat and keep the sauce covered.

For The French Toast

- ¼ cup chickpea flour
- ½ teaspoon ground cinnamon
- ½ teaspoon vanilla extract
- 2 tablespoons brown sugar

- ¾ cup plant-based milk
- 1 tablespoon Earth Balance vegan butter
- 4 to 6 slices whole-grain bread

Directions:

1. In a medium mixing bowl, whisk together the chickpea flour, cinnamon, vanilla, brown sugar, and ¾ cup of milk.
2. Heat a skillet over medium heat, then add the butter and allow it to melt. While the butter is melting, dip the bread slices into the chickpea mixture. Turn to coat both sides, shake off any excess batter, and place the bread in the hot skillet.
3. Cook until golden brown; then flip to cook the other side.
4. Remove the toast from the skillet and transfer to a plate. Top with the peach mixture and a dollop of whipped cream. Repeat with all of the remaining bread slices. Serve immediately.

Smoky Grits with Cajun "Butter" and Roasted Vegetables

Southern cuisine is known for grits. Some like them sweet, while others, like me, like them savory. Grits are basically a less-starchy corn dried and ground to make tiny granules. When I was growing up, grits and Cream of Wheat were the two main hot cereals I could almost always find in the cabinet. My recipe is a savory flavor-packed bowl of goodness!

Makes 2servings

Ingredients:

- 1 cup diced zucchini
- 1 cup diced yellow squash
- 8 stems asparagus, cut into 6-inch pieces
- ½ cup button mushrooms, sliced thick
- ½ red onion, diced
- ½ cup diced bell peppers
- 2 tablespoons grapeseed or sunflower oil
- 3 pinches sea salt, divided
- 3 cups water
- 3 cups plant-based milk
- 1½ cups quick grits
- ½ teaspoon liquid smoke
- 3 tablespoons Earth Balance vegan butter
- 1½ teaspoons Creole Cajun Seasoning

Directions:

1. Preheat the oven to 425°F. Line a baking pan with parchment paper.
2. In a medium mixing bowl, stir together the zucchini, yellow squash, asparagus, mushrooms, onion, bell peppers, oil, and 1 pinch of salt.
3. Spread the veggies on the lined baking pan and roast for 10 to 12 minutes.
4. In a medium saucepan, bring the water and milk to a boil. Add the remaining 2 pinches of salt; then slowly add the grits, stirring continuously. Cover and reduce the heat to low. Stir occasionally for 5 to 6 minutes. The grits will be done when they become thick and creamy.
5. Once the grits are soft, turn off the heat, add the liquid smoke, stir, and cover.
6. Remove the veggies from the oven and allow to cool.
7. In a small saucepan over low heat, melt the butter, add the Cajun seasoning, and stir.

8. To serve, spoon the grits into a bowl and top with the roasted veggies and Cajun butter.

Smoky Tempeh Bacon

Believe me, you won't miss regular bacon after tasting this vegan version. I usually have to make a double batch of these babies, because they are gone before I can even add them to a breakfast sandwich. You can swap out the tempeh if you're trying to stay away from soy and use unsweetened coconut flakes, eggplant slices, or king oyster mushrooms instead. This bacon is a great addition to almost any recipe and is especially great as a side dish with waffles or corn cakes.

Makes 2servings

Ingredients:

- 1 (8-ounce) package tempeh
- ¼ cup tamari
- ¼ cup maple syrup
- 1½ tablespoons liquid smoke

Directions:

1. Preheat the oven to 400°F.
2. Slice the tempeh into ½-inch-thick strips and place them in an 8-by-10-inch baking pan.
3. In a medium bowl, whisk together the tamari, maple syrup, and liquid smoke.
4. Pour the marinade over the tempeh, and let sit for 10 minutes, turning each piece after 5 minutes so that both sides are coated.
5. Bake for 6 minutes, then turn each piece of tempeh over and bake for another 6 minutes.
6. Remove from the oven and let cool for 2 to 3 minutes before serving.

Peanut Butter Green Smoothie Bowl

I have smoothies most days for breakfast. They are not only satisfying but also a great way to have something quick, healthy, and protein-packed that will fuel you for hours. A smoothie bowl is just a thicker smoothie poured into a bowl and topped with a variety of sliced fruit, granola, nuts, and seeds.

Makes 2 servings

Ingredients:

- 2 cups coconut milk
- 2 ripe bananas
- 8 pitted dates
- 1 ripe avocado
- 2 handfuls spinach or baby kale
- 4 tablespoons peanut butter
- 2 tablespoons hemp hearts
- 1½ to 2 cups ice

Directions:

1. Place all the ingredients in a high-powered blender and blend on medium-high for 2 to 3 minutes or until well combined.
2. Pour the smoothie into a medium serving bowl and top with your choice of toppings.

Biscuits and Gravy

This recipe is a true southern classic. Fresh biscuits appeared regularly in my nana's house, and we loved it when she would serve them with sausage gravy. When veganizing this recipe, I knew I needed to make sure that the buttery, crispy outside and warm, fluffy inside were carried over from Nana's recipe. Enjoy!

Makes 2servings

Ingredients:

- 4½ tablespoons sunflower oil
- ½ teaspoon salt
- ½ teaspoon freshly ground black pepper
- 1½ teaspoons dried thyme
- 2 teaspoons granulated garlic
- 1 teaspoon onion powder
- 4½ tablespoons unbleached all-purpose flour
- 3 cups water or plant-based milk
- 1 batch Buttermilk Biscuits
- 2 tablespoons chopped flat-leaf parsley

Directions:

1. In a medium sauté pan, heat the oil over medium-high heat; then add the salt, black pepper, thyme, granulated garlic, and onion powder and stir to combine. Turn the heat down to low and sauté for 3 to 5 minutes.
2. Stir in the flour until well combined and allow to lightly brown; then add the water and stir.
3. Cook for 5 to 8 minutes, to desired thickness.
4. Plate the biscuits, pour the gravy over the top, and garnish with the parsley to serve.

Sweet Potato Quinoa Pancakes

The addition of sweet potato Serves:these pancakes extra moist, while adding quinoa gives you a protein and fiber boost to start your day. This recipe is a great way to use leftover sweet potatoes and quinoa, which also helps cut down on cooking time. Add a side of Smoky Tempeh Bacon or Maple-Sage Breakfast Sausage for a real southern breakfast experience.

Makes 2servings

Ingredients:

- 1 cup gluten-free flour
- ⅓ cup sweet potato purée
- 1 tablespoon grapeseed or sunflower oil
- ¾ tablespoon baking powder
- ½ teaspoon cinnamon
- 1 tablespoon flax meal
- ½ teaspoon vanilla extract
- ½ cup cooked quinoa
- 1½ teaspoons agave nectar
- Pinch sea salt
- Nonstick cooking spray

Directions:

1. Preheat the oven to the lowest setting, about 140°F.
2. In a medium mixing bowl, whisk together all the ingredientsexcept the cooking spray until well combined. Set aside for 5 minutes.
3. Heat a griddle or nonstick pan and use the cooking spray to evenly coat the surface.
4. Once the griddle is nice and hot, spoon about ⅓ cup of the pancake mixture onto it to form each pancake. Usually 3 pancakes can cook at a time.
5. When the pancakes begin to form air bubbles, usually after about 4 minutes, check that the bottoms are golden brown; then flip and allow to cook for another 3 to 4 minutes.
6. Transfer the pancakes to the oven to keep warm while you finish cooking the remaining pancakes.

Farmhouse Scramble

This hearty, protein-packed scramble is a wonderful replacement for scrambled eggs and reminds me of the weekend breakfasts we made growing up. Eggs are inexpensive, but tofu is even cheaper and Serves:a delicious meal that will keep you full for hours.

Makes 2servings

Ingredients:

For The Seasoning Blend

- 1 teaspoon turmeric
- ½ teaspoon smoked paprika
- 1 teaspoon granulated garlic
- ½ teaspoon onion powder
- ¼ teaspoon freshly ground black pepper
- 1 teaspoon cumin
- ½ teaspoon curry powder
- ¼ teaspoon chili powder

For The Scramble

- 1 tablespoon tamari
- 1 (16-ounce) package firm tofu, drained
- 1 tablespoon grapeseed oil
- ⅓ cup red onions, diced
- ⅓ cup colored bell peppers, diced
- 6 shiitake mushrooms, thinly sliced
- 1 garlic clove, minced
- ⅓ cup roughly chopped kale
- ⅓ cup roughly chopped Swiss chard

Directions:

1. Mix together the turmeric, paprika, granulated garlic, onion powder, black pepper, cumin, curry powder, and chili powder. Set the seasoning mix aside.
2. In a medium bowl, mash the drained tofu with a masher or by hand to make crumbles.
3. After the tofu is crumbled, add the seasoning mixture. Mix well and set aside.
4. In a medium sauté pan over medium-high heat, heat the oil; then add the onions, bell peppers, and mushrooms and stir.
5. Allow the vegetables to cook for 3 to 4 minutes, until the onions are slightly translucent; then add the garlic and tamari, and stir. Allow to cook for 1 minute.

6. Add the seasoned tofu. Cook, stirring often, for a few minutes. Then add the kale and Swiss chard and stir.

7. Cook for 4 to 5 minutes, or until the kale has softened. Remove from the heat and serve.

Maple-Sage Breakfast Sausage

You won't believe how simple and tasty these breakfast sausages are! They take me on a trip down memory lane. When I was a child, my father would make some amazing dishes with textured vegetable protein (TVP), and I loved to watch him create magic in the kitchen with these little granules. TVP also can be used to replace ground beef in tacos, chili, or pasta dishes. I used TVP even when I wasn't vegan, and people never knew they were eating a meatless dish. You can find TVP in the health food section in most grocery stores. Look for Bob's Red Mill products, as they are usually grouped together. If you're unable to locate it at your grocery store, you can order it online.

Makes 2servings

Ingredients:

- Nonstick cooking spray
- ¾ cup textured vegetable protein (TVP)
- ¾ cup boiling hot water
- 3 tablespoons flax meal
- ⅓ cup water
- ¼ cup nutritional yeast
- 4 tablespoons maple syrup
- 1 teaspoon dried thyme
- 2 to 3 teaspoons ground sage
- 1 tablespoon garlic powder
- 1 teaspoon onion powder
- Pinch cayenne pepper
- 2 tablespoons tamari
- ¼ cup flour, plus more as needed

Directions:

1. Preheat the oven to 400°F. Line a baking pan with parchment paper or coat with cooking spray.
2. In a medium bowl, cover the TVP with the hot water and stir. Cover and set aside for 5 minutes.
3. In a small bowl, mix the flax meal and ⅓ cup water with a fork or whisk to create a "flax egg." Let the mixture sit for 5 to 7 minutes to thicken.
4. Uncover the TVP and stir with a large spoon, then add the nutritional yeast, maple syrup, thyme, sage, garlic powder, onion powder, cayenne pepper, tamari, and flour, along with the flax egg mixture.

5. Stir the mixture for 1 to 2 minutes, then test your mixture by taking about 1 tablespoon and forming it into a ball in your hands. The mixture should not be too loose. If it is, add a little more flour and mix again.
6. Remove the lid from a large mason jar. Hold the lid upside down in the palm of your hand and pack it tightly with the TVP mixture, making sure it is not overflowing and has a smooth surface.
7. Turn the packed lid over onto the prepared baking pan and lightly push through the lid hole to release the patty.
8. Repeat this process to make a total of 8 patties, then place the baking pan into the oven and bake for 6 to 7 minutes. Turn the patties over and bake for another 6 to 7 minutes.
9. The patties are ready when they are browned and slightly crispy. Remove from the oven, and let cool for 2 to 3 minutes before serving.

Chapter 4: Appetizers

Crab Cakes

Crab cakes make scrumptious appetizers and are popular items on restaurant menus all over, from the East Coast to Kansas. This recipe is super easy and delicious to prepare. You can try these crab cakes to serve to friends on a busy weeknight, or for a spectacular weekend get-together.

Makes 2servings

Ingredients:

- ½ cup mayonnaise
- 1 large egg, lightly beaten
- 1 tablespoon Dijon mustard
- 1 tablespoon Worcestershire sauce
- ½ tablespoon hot sauce
- 1 pound fresh lump crabmeat, drained
- 1 cup crushed saltines (20 crackers)
- 1 quart vegetable oil
- Tartar sauce (to serve)

Directions:

1. Line a baking sheet with waxed paper.
2. In a mixing bowl, stir the mayonnaise, egg, mustard, Worcestershire sauce, and hot sauce together.
3. Fold in the crabmeat and the saltines, and allow the mixture to rest for 5 minutes.
4. Shape the mixture into 8 patties, and place them on the baking sheet, cover, and chill for an hour.
5. Heat a few tablespoons of oil in a frying pan, and fry the crab cakes over medium heat for 3 to 4 minutes on each side until golden.
6. Place the fried patties on paper towels to allow the oil to drain.
7. Serve the crab cakes while they are still hot along with tartar sauce if desired.

Bang Bang Shrimp

Bang Bang shrimp are the best appetizers for hot Southern nights. If you are still craving the famous appetizer from your favorite chain restaurant, this Bang Bang Shrimp recipe is the one to go for. Now you can make delicious shrimp with just the right amount of kick! If you want, use more of the chili sauce to give it a bit more spice.

Makes 2 servings

Ingredients:

- 1 pound shrimp, shelled and deveined
- ½ cup mayonnaise
- ¼ cup Thai sweet chili sauce
- 3-5 drops of hot sauce
- ½ to ¾ cup cornstarch to coat the shrimp
- Oil for deep frying
- Scallions, chopped, for garnish

Directions:

1. In a small bowl, mix the mayonnaise and the sauces together to prepare the coating.
2. Dip the shrimp in the sauce and then gently bread in the cornstarch.
3. Preheat the oil in the deep fryer to 350°F.
4. Fry the shrimp until they turn lightly golden, about one minute.
5. Drain the shrimp on a paper towel.
6. Coat the shrimp with the sauces, and serve with chopped scallions to garnish.

Fried Green Tomatoes

You can't have Southern cuisine without fried green tomatoes!

Makes 2servings

Ingredients:

- 1 large egg
- 4 tablespoons milk
- Vegetable olive oil
- 1 cup cornmeal
- 1 cup all-purpose flour
- 3 large green tomatoes, sliced ¼-inch thick
- Ranch dressing for dipping

Directions:

1. In a small bowl, combine the egg and milk, and whisk.
2. In a medium-sized bowl, mix the flour and cornmeal.
3. In a heavy and deep skillet, heat oil over medium heat. The oil should cover the bottom of the skillet with about ½ inch in depth.
4. Dredge the tomato slices in the egg mixture followed by the cornmeal mixture, and place the slices in hot oil. Don't overcrowd the skillet. Cook and turn until the tomatoes are golden brown on both sides, about 1-3 minutes per side.
5. Place the fried tomatoes on a plate covered with paper towels to catch the excess oil.
6. Serve warm with your favorite dipping sauce such as a ranch dressing.

Coconut Shrimp

If you are looking for great coconut shrimp, this delectable recipe is just for you. Large juicy shrimp dipped in batter and then in a mixture of coconut and curry powder, and deep-fried to perfection make great appetizers and snacks. This juicy, delicious dish is incredibly easy to make and your guests will be craving more.

Makes 2servings

Ingredients:

- 1 cup flour
- 2 pounds large shrimp
- ½ teaspoon salt
- ½ teaspoon sugar
- 1 egg, lightly beaten

- 2 tablespoons vegetable oil
- 2/3 cup grated coconut
- 1 ½ teaspoon curry powder
- 1 cup ice water
- Hot sauce, for serving

Directions:

1. Shell and devein the shrimp, leaving the tail intact.
2. In a medium-sized bowl, combine the egg, sugar, salt, vegetable oil, ice water, and flour, and beat the mixture until it is smooth.
3. In a separate bowl, mix the coconut and curry powder.
4. Dip the shrimp into the batter and then into the coconut mixture.
5. Fry the coconut shrimp in hot fat until it turns golden brown on both sides.
6. Serve the shrimp with some hot sauce, if desired.

Deep-Fried Dill Pickles

If you are looking for a refreshing snack, look no further than this recipe. These tangy, crispy, and extremely delicious deep-fried dill pickles are among the most delicious appetizers out there. Feel free to double the amount of cayenne pepper if you like the pickles to be spicier.

Makes 2servings

Ingredients:

- 2 large eggs
- 1 cup buttermilk
- ½ teaspoon hot sauce
- 1 ½ teaspoons black pepper, separated
- 1 ¼ teaspoons salt, separated
- 2 ¼ cups all-purpose flour, separated

- 1 cup cornmeal
- 1 teaspoon cayenne pepper
- 1 jar dill pickle slices
- Vegetable oil for frying
- Ranch dressing, or your choice of dip, to serve

Directions:

1. In a medium-sized bowl, combine the eggs, buttermilk, hot sauce, ¼ cup flour, black pepper, cayenne pepper, and ¼ teaspoon of salt.
2. In another shallow bowl, combine the remaining 2 cups of flour, cornmeal, and the remaining 1 teaspoon of salt and black pepper.
3. Preheat the oil in the deep fryer to 375°F.
4. Remove the pickle slices from the jar and blot them dry with a paper towel.
5. Dip the pickle slices first into the buttermilk mixture and then in the cornmeal mixture.
6. Deep fry the pickles until they appear golden brown, this will take 1 to 2 minutes.
7. Drain the deep-fried pickles on a paper towel to get rid of the excess oil.
8. Serve with a dish of ranch dressing for dipping.

Pinto Beans

Hearty, flavorful pinto beans make an excellent side dish and are good with just about everything. This Southern Style staple is sure to remind you of sunny afternoon barbecues. Sometimes, all you need is a good old hearty bowl of Pinto beans to fill you to the brim. The flourish of thyme and oregano add an exotic aroma and taste.

Makes 2servings

Ingredients:

- 2 cups dried pinto beans
- 4 cups of chicken broth
- ¼ pound cooked ham, shredded
- 1 teaspoon black pepper
- ½ teaspoon thyme
- 2 teaspoons salt
- ½ teaspoon garlic powder
- ½ teaspoon dried oregano
- ¼ teaspoon chili powder
- ¼ teaspoon ground cumin
- 3 bay leaves

Directions:

1. Soak the beans in water overnight, or for at least 6 to 8 hours
2. The following day, drain the beans and discard the water, and place the beans in a slow cooker with all the other ingredients.
3. Cook the mixture on low for 10 hours, or on high for 5 hours
4. After the mixture has finished cooking, take 2 cups of the bean soup and puree, using a food processor or blender.
5. Add the puree back to the beans, and cook on high for at least 30 minutes. This will thicken the soup.
6. Remove the beans from the slow cooker and serve.

Fried Shrimp

If you are in the mood for some good old-fashioned fried shrimp, you will never believe how easy it is to make them. In this delectable recipe, shrimp will be coated with batter and then deep-fried to crunchy perfection.

Makes 2servings

Ingredients:

- 3 cups of large, deveined and peeled shrimp
- Salt and pepper
- 1 egg, beaten
- ½ cup yellow cornmeal
- ½ teaspoon baking powder
- ½ cup half and half cream
- ½ cup buttermilk
- 1 teaspoons salt
- ¼ teaspoon black pepper
- ½ teaspoon baking powder
- ½ teaspoon all-purpose flour
- Oil to fry your shrimp
- ¼ teaspoon pepper

Directions:

1. Start by seasoning generously your shrimp with some salt and pepper and then leave them to sit at room temperature for 10 to 15 minutes.
2. Combine the eggs, cornmeal, baking powder, cream, buttermilk, salt, pepper, baking powder, and flour in a mixing bowl and mix until well blended and smooth.
3. Heat the oil in the deep fryer until it reaches 350°F.
4. Dip the shrimp in the batter to coat evenly.
5. Fry the shrimp until they are golden. This will take around 2 minutes.
6. Serve the shrimp hot, with your favorite sauce.

Corn Chowder

You just can't resist trying your hand at Corn Chowder. This hearty soup can carry a meal at the end of summer. With its rich corn and bacon, this creamy recipe is the perfect Southern Styled Corn Chowder.

Makes 2servings

Ingredients:

- 4 ounces chopped bacon
- ½ cup celery, finely chopped
- ½ cup carrots, finely chopped
- 1 cup onions, finely chopped
- 2 tablespoons garlic, minced
- ¼ cup all-purpose flour
- 2 quarts chicken stock
- 1 ½ cups russet potatoes, cubed and peeled
- 1 cup heavy cream
- 5 cups kernel corn
- ¾ cup red bell peppers, finely chopped
- 1 tablespoon salt
- ¼ teaspoon cayenne pepper
- Finely chopped parsley for garnishing

Directions:

1. Place an 8-quart stockpot over medium heat and allow the bacon to cook until it is crispy. This should take about 5 minutes.
2. When the bacon is cooked, remove it to drain on a paper towel.
3. To the stockpot, add the onions, carrots, and celery and allow the mixture to cook, stirring occasionally, until it is soft, about 5 minutes.
4. Add garlic, bell peppers, and corn to the pot and allow cook for 10 minutes, stirring often.
5. Sprinkle the flour over the vegetables, and stir constantly for 5 minutes. Slowly pour in the chicken stock, mixing to combine all the ingredients. You may use a whisk if necessary to break up the lumps if any have formed.
6. Add the potatoes and bring the mixture to a boil, and cook for at least 20 minutes, until the potatoes are fork-tender.
7. Finally, add salt, cayenne pepper, and stir in the cream.
8. Garnish with some bacon and fresh parsley. Enjoy!

Hot Corn Dip

This spicy and cheesy corn dip with tortillas Serves:a perfect combination. Fall in love with this easy dip that takes less than five minutes to put together.

Makes 2servings

Ingredients:

- 2 cups corn kernel
- ½ cup diced onion
- 2 tablespoons mayonnaise
- 1 ½ tablespoons butter
- 1 clove garlic, minced
- 1-2 jalapenos, seeded and diced
- ¼ teaspoon seasoned salt
- ¾ cup sharp cheddar cheese, shredded
- ½ cup Monterey Jack Cheese, shredded
- ¼ teaspoon chili powder
- 4 tablespoons cream cheese
- 1 green onion, sliced
- Tortilla chips for dipping
- Cooking spray

Directions:

1. Preheat oven to 375°F.
2. In a skillet, melt butter, and add corn, onion, and jalapeño. Sauté for 3 minutes.
3. Add garlic and continue to sauté for 1 to 2 more minutes.
4. Remove the mixture from heat and allow the mixture to cool for a few minutes before adding all the remaining ingredients. Stir to combine.
5. Transfer to a baking dish coated with cooking spray, and bake for 20 minutes, until the cheese bubbles.
6. Serve with tortilla chips for dipping.

Southern Pimento Cheese

This delicious recipe for Pimento cheese can be used for making yummy grilled sandwiches, or as a spread for crackers. Plus, your family will love the spicy kick! We bet the unique combination of creamy, spicy, and salty flavors used in this recipe is good enough to make your friends and family swoon. Don't be surprised if you are bombarded with requests for this treat at every get-together!

Makes 2servings

Ingredients:

- 2 cups shredded cheddar cheese
- ½ cup mayonnaise
- ¼ teaspoon garlic powder
- ¼ teaspoon ground cayenne powder
- 8 ounces cream cheese
- 1 jalapeno pepper, minced
- ½ teaspoon onion powder
- 1 jar diced pimentos, drained
- Salt and pepper to taste
- Crackers or baguette, to serve

Directions:

1. In the bowl of a mixer, place the mayonnaise, garlic powder, onion powder, cheddar cheese, cream cheese, cayenne pepper, pimentos, and jalapeño.
2. Mix all the ingredients at medium speed until thoroughly combined.
3. Season the mixture with salt and pepper, and transfer to a clean bowl.
4. Serve the pimento cheese with crackers or slices of baguette.

Pineapple Cream Cheese Salad

Whipped cream, pineapple, and cream cheese will set the mood for this awesome salad you can prepare within minutes. This festive salad is one of the treats that help make Christmas so special. Remember, salads cannot get creamier, cooler, or more refreshing than this.

Makes 2servings

Ingredients:

- ½ cup mayonnaise
- 1 cup whipped cream
- 1 package lemon gelatin
- 1 can crushed pineapple
- 1 cup cream cheese
- 1 cup water
- ⅓ cup chopped walnuts

Directions:

1. In a medium-sized bowl combine the whipped cream and mayonnaise and then place in the refrigerator. Allow the mixture to cool for an hour.
2. Combine the pineapple and water in a saucepan and bring to a boil. Reduce heat to low.
3. Add the lemon gelatin to the mixture, stir continuously until dissolved completely, and then allow it to cool.
4. Before the gelatin sets, add the whipped cream mixture together with the cream cheese. Stir to combine well. Place in the refrigerator for 1-2 hours, or until set.
5. Sprinkle the walnuts on top. Serve chilled.

Shrimp and Grits

Shrimp and grits make a great appetizer; in fact, they take Southern snacks to the next level. They are sometimes called breakfast shrimp but taste great at any time of the day. Now you can use this quick and easy shrimp and grits recipe to wow your family at the dinner or impress guests at weekend events.

Makes 2servings

Ingredients:

- 1 ½ pounds peeled and deveined shrimp
- ½ teaspoon hot sauce
- 3 tablespoons fresh lemon juice
- 2 bacon slices, chopped
- ½ cup chopped green onions, plus a few tablespoons for serving
- 1 ½ cup green bell pepper, chopped
- 1 cup chicken broth
- 5 cups water
- 1 tablespoon butter
- 1 teaspoon salt
- 1 ½ cups chopped grits
- 1 ½ teaspoons minced garlic
- ¾ cup shredded cheddar cheese

Directions:

1. In a medium-sized bowl, combine the shrimp, hot sauce, and lemon juice.
2. Cook bacon in a skillet over medium heat until nice and crisp.
3. Add ½ cup green onions, bell pepper, and garlic to the pan and allow it to cook for 5 minutes until tender, stirring occasionally.
4. Stir in the broth, shrimp mixture, and ¼ cup of green onions, and allow the mixture to cook for 5 minutes until the shrimp have completely cooked.
5. In another saucepan, bring the water to a boil and then stir in the grits.
6. Lower the heat to low and allow it to simmer, covered, for 5 minutes until the mixture has thickened.
7. Stir in butter and add salt to taste.
8. Serve the shrimp over the grits, with shredded cheese and green onion sprinkled on top.

Chapter 5: Main Entrées

Jambalaya

If you are craving a New Orleans classic, this recipe for Jambalaya is the perfect option for you. This spicy rice is all you need to fill yourself to the brim. Treat your taste buds to deep flavors with this authentic Jambalaya recipe any time you want. After all, you just cannot resist the aroma of sautéed aromatic onion, celery, and peppers, with herbs, garlic, and spices.

Makes 2servings

Ingredients:

- 1 pound chicken breast, diced
- 1 medium-sized yellow onion, chopped
- 2 tablespoons butter
- ½ pound andouille sausage, sliced in ¼ inch slices
- 1 green bell pepper, diced
- 1 stalk celery, diced
- 3 cloves of garlic, minced
- 2 teaspoons hot sauce
- 2 cups chicken or fish broth
- 1 teaspoon Worcestershire sauce
- 1 can diced tomatoes
- 2 bay leaves
- ¾ teaspoon salt
- ½ teaspoon black pepper each
- ½ pound raw shrimp, deveined
- 2 tablespoons Creole seasoning
- 1 cup long-grain rice
- 4 green onions, thinly sliced, for garnish

Directions:

1. Combine all the spices for the Creole seasoning and place it in a clean coffee grinder. Grind until you have a fine powder, and store the powder in an airtight jar.
2. Place the chicken in a large bowl and sprinkle with 1 tablespoon of the Creole seasoning. Set it aside to rest.
3. Place a large skillet on medium-high heat and melt the butter.
4. Cook the chicken and the sausage until browned, and drain excess fat.
5. Add the bell pepper, garlic, onion, and celery, and cook for 4 minutes.
6. Add the rice, and the remaining tablespoon of Creole seasoning, diced tomatoes, hot sauce, salt, black pepper, and Worcestershire sauce, and stir the mixture until it is thoroughly combined.

7. Add the chicken broth and bay leaves, and bring the mixture to a boil. Reduce the heat to medium-low, cover the pot, and allow it to simmer for 15 minutes. Give it a stir around the halfway point.
8. Finally, add the shrimp, cover, and then allow the Jambalaya to simmer for another 10 minutes until the rice turns tender and thoroughly cooked.
9. Place in a serving dish and enjoy with a sprinkle of green onions, while it is still hot!

Grandma's Fried Chicken

Nothing can compete with Southern Fried Chicken, and this recipe is great for feeding a crowd. Simply kick back, enjoy, and relax as you devour this delicious meal. Those of you who want to add a satisfying twist to this classic can pour in a little extra hot sauce.

Makes 2servings

Ingredients:

- 1 chicken (2-3 pounds), cut into 8 pieces

Marinade

- 4 cups buttermilk
- 1 teaspoon (or more) hot sauce

Dredging Mixture

- 1 teaspoon garlic powder
- 1 teaspoon cayenne pepper (or more if you like spicier)
- 1 teaspoon salt
- 1 teaspoon black pepper

- Peanut oil for frying (enough to cover the chicken in the saucepan)
- Dipping sauce for serving

- 1 teaspoon salt
- 1 teaspoon black pepper

- 1 teaspoon cumin
- 1 teaspoon dry thyme
- 1 teaspoon baking powder
- 2½ cups all-purpose flour

Directions:

1. In a large mixing bowl, add the buttermilk, hot sauce, salt, and black pepper. Whisk to combine well. Add the chicken pieces. The buttermilk mixture should cover the chicken. Using your hands, make sure the chicken pieces are well covered in buttermilk. Refrigerate for at least 3 hours and up to 12 hours. Remove the chicken from the refrigerator at least 1 hour before cooking to bring it to room temperature.
2. In a large, deep pot, heat the peanut oil to 350°F. You can also use a deep cast-iron skillet, filled to the ¾ with the oil.
3. Prepare the dredging mixture in a shallow bowl by adding all the ingredientsand mixing well.

4. Remove the chicken pieces from the buttermilk mixture and dredge into the flour one piece at a time. Shake gently to remove excess flout. Carefully lower it into the hot oil with a slotted spoon.

5. Do not crowd all the chicken pieces together; cook half the chicken at a time until crispy and brown, about 15 minutes. Turn the chicken over after 7 or 8 minutes. Once cooked, remove the chicken pieces with a slotted spoon and drain on paper towels.

6. To check the doneness of the chicken, poke the chicken with a fork on the thickest part of the chicken to make sure the juices run clear or that the internal temperature should read at least 165°F on an instant reading meat thermometer when inserted in the thickest part of the chicken piece without touching a bone.

7. Enjoy while hot, with the dipping sauce of your choice!

Southern Fried Pork Chops

Looking for a tender, juicy pork chop recipe that turns out perfectly every time? Well, you need to look no further. Southern-fried pork chops are simple to make, yet so delicious. You can serve them for lunch, dinner, or even as a late brunch.

Makes 2servings

Ingredients:

- 4 thin-cut, bone-in pork chops
- 1 cup buttermilk
- Vegetable oil for frying
- 1 cup self-rising flour
- Seasoned salt and pepper to taste

Directions:

1. Season each side of the pork with seasoned salt and pepper.
2. Pour the buttermilk into a shallow bowl, and cover a plate or pie pan with flour.
3. Dip the pork chops first onto the buttermilk and then coat with the flour evenly on both sides.
4. Refrigerate for 30 minutes.
5. Heat a few tablespoons of oil in a large pan over high heat, enough to cook four chops at a time.
6. Fry the pork chops, making sure each side is browned, about 8 minutes per side.

Crawfish Pie

This delicious Southern-style pie is loaded with the goodness of vegetables that even the pickiest eaters will enjoy. A little hint of heat from cayenne pepper can give your taste buds an exciting treat. There's no special day to try this recipe — any time is good!

Makes 2servings

Ingredients:

- ¼ cup butter
- ½ cup celery, chopped
- 1 cup onion, chopped
- ½ cup green pepper, chopped
- 1 ½ teaspoons salt
- 1 prepared deep-dish pie crust, 9 inch
- 1 cup diced tomatoes
- ½ teaspoon ground cayenne pepper
- 2 tablespoons all-purpose flour
- 1/8 teaspoon white pepper
- 12 ounces peeled crawfish tails
- 1 cup water

Directions:

1. Line the deep-dish pie plate with the pie crust, and set aside.
2. In a large skillet, melt the butter over medium heat, and stir in the celery, onion, green pepper, salt, cayenne pepper, and white pepper, and cook until the vegetables are tender, about 5 minutes.
3. Stir in the tomatoes and the crawfish, reduce the heat, and allow the mixture to cook for 3 minutes to blend the flavors. Stir occasionally.
4. In a large bowl, whisk the flour and water together until smooth, pour the mixture into the skillet.
5. Stir the filling and bring it to a simmer, stirring until the mixture thickens.
6. Remove the mixture from the heat and allow it to rest 20 to 30 minutes
7. Preheat the oven to 400°F.
8. Pour the filling into the prepared pie crust, and bake it in the oven until the crust turns golden brown and the filling starts to bubble, 30 to 40 minutes.
9. Take the pie out of the oven and allow it to cool for 10 minutes before serving.

Barbecue Pulled Pork Sandwiches

These easy (only three ingredients !) and delicious barbecue pulled pork sandwiches make a heavenly meal that will satisfy your Southern cravings. Pork slow-cooked in spices and sauce is great for lunch or dinner on any day. In fact, you can put it on before going out to work – this juicy pork will be ready when you get home.

Makes 2servings

Ingredients:

- 1 can beef broth
- 1 bottle barbecue sauce
- 3 pounds boneless pork ribs
- 12 Buns
- Favorite toppings such as tomatoes and coleslaw
- French fries, for serving

Directions:

1. Pour the beef broth into a slow cooker and add the pork ribs. Cook on high heat for 4 hours, until the meat is tender and shreds easily.
2. Preheat the oven to 350°F.
3. Place the shredded pork in a cast-iron skillet or Dutch oven and stir in the barbecue sauce.
4. Bake the pork in the oven for 30 minutes until it is properly heated through.
5. Place a generous amount of the pulled pork on a bun, top with toppings. Serve with French fries if desired.

Southern Chicken Fried Steak

A classic of every dinner restaurant in the Southern states. Crispy and juicy at the same time, the fried chicken "steaks" will become a favorite of your family.

Makes 2servings

Ingredients:

- 2 cups all-purpose flour
- 6 skinless and boneless chicken breasts
- ¼ cup oil for frying
- 1 teaspoon dry oregano
- ½ teaspoon cumin
- ½ teaspoon paprika
- 1-2 pinches cayenne pepper, to taste
- Salt and pepper to taste
- 2 eggs
- Hot sauce for serving

Directions:

1. In a large bowl, combine the flour with the oregano, cumin, paprika, cayenne, salt, and pepper.
2. In another bowl, beat the eggs.
3. Between 2 plastic wrap paper, pound each chicken breast until you get them to about ½ inch thick. Try to make the cutlets even in size.
4. Coat each chicken cutlet first in the flour mixture, then dip into egg, followed by another coat in the flour mixture.
5. In a skillet, heat oil over medium-high heat. Place veal cutlets into hot oil and fry until each side is browned, about 5 minutes per side.
6. Serve with a side of hot sauce.

Louisiana Red Bean and Rice

This authentic recipe is a favorite from Louisiana. No matter when you make it, it will be impossible for you to keep your hands off it. Add a splash of cider vinegar and you will be amazed by the delicious flavor. Ask any person who grew up in Louisiana, they'll tell you how this simple recipe has changed the dimensions of Southern cuisine.

Makes 2servings

Ingredients:

- 1 pound andouille sausage, sliced
- 1 pound kidney beans
- ¼ cup olive oil
- 1 large onion, chopped
- 1 green bell pepper, chopped
- 2 celery stalks, chopped
- 2 tablespoons garlic, minced
- ½ teaspoon cayenne pepper
- 1 tablespoon dried parsley
- ¼ teaspoon dried sage
- 1 teaspoon dried thyme
- 1 teaspoon Cajun seasoning
- 2 cups long-grain white rice
- 4 cups beef broth
- 6 cups water
- 2 bay leaves

Directions:

1. Soak the beans in water in a large saucepan overnight.
2. In a medium-sized skillet, heat the oil over medium heat, and sauté onion, celery, bell pepper, and garlic in olive oil for 3 to 4 minutes
3. Rinse the beans and cover them with 6 cups of water.
4. Add cooked vegetables to the beans, and stir in the cayenne pepper, parsley, sage, thyme, bay leaves, and Cajun seasoning.
5. Bring the mixture to a boil, and reduce the heat to medium-low, and simmer for 2 ½ hours.
6. Stir the sausage into the beans and allow it to simmer for 30 minutes.
7. In a saucepan, boil 4 cups of beef broth, and add the rice. Reduce the heat, cover it, and allow it to simmer for 20 minutes. You can also use a rice cooker.
8. Serve the bean mixture over the hot rice.

Double Crust Chicken Pot Pie

Want to discover a classic Southern secret? Well, this recipe is the one you need to check out. The Double Crust Chicken pot pie is enough to dazzle your guests and bring the Southern atmosphere home. The golden crust will win you rave reviews at the dinner table.

Makes 2 servings

Ingredients:

- 1 large egg
- 1 can chicken broth
- ½ cup butter
- ½ cup all-purpose flour
- 2 medium leeks, sliced
- 1 cup carrots, cut in matchsticks
- 3 cups of cooked chicken, chopped
- ½ teaspoon salt
- ½ teaspoon ground pepper
- 1 ½ cups frozen cubed hash browns with onions and peppers
- ⅓ cup chopped parsley
- 1 package of puff pastry

Directions:

1. Preheat the oven to 375°F.
2. In a large skillet, heat the butter over medium heat, add the leeks and sauté for 3 minutes.
3. Sprinkle flour over the mixture, and continue to stir constantly for 3 minutes.
4. Whisking constantly, blend in the chicken broth and bring the mixture to a boil.
5. Remove from the heat, and add the chicken, carrots, parsley, salt, pepper, hash browns, and stir to combine.
6. Coat a clean surface with flour, and roll each pastry sheet into a 12x10 inch rectangle.
7. Fit the sheet into a 9-inch pie plate, making sure the narrow sides cover the rim of the pie plate. Scoop in the chicken mixture into the pastry.
8. Place the remaining pastry sheet over the chicken mixture in the opposite direction of the bottom sheet
9. Tuck and press the edges around the dish, and press the edges with a fork to seal the crust. Trim the excess.
10. In a separate bowl, whisk a large egg with 1 tablespoon of water, and brush the mixture over the top of the pie.

11. Bake the pie in the oven at 375°F on the middle rack of the oven for 55 to 60 minutes until the crust starts to brown.
12. Let the pie rest for about 15 minutes before serving.

Chunky Beef Chili

This hearty bowl of chunky chili is just what you need to remind you of the traditional American South chili seasonings.

Makes 2servings

Ingredients:

- 4 pounds boneless chuck roast, cubed
- 2 6 oz. cans of tomato paste
- 2 15 oz. cans tomato sauce
- 2 tablespoons chili powder
- 2 teaspoons granulated garlic
- 1 teaspoon ground cumin
- 1 teaspoon ground oregano
- 1 teaspoon salt
- ½ teaspoon onion powder
- ½ teaspoon ground black pepper
- ¼ teaspoon ground red pepper
- 1 teaspoon paprika

Directions:

1. Brown the meat in batches in a Dutch oven over medium-high heat.
2. Remove the meat from the pot, but keep the drippings in the pot. Add chili powder and cook for 2 minutes, stirring constantly.
3. Place the beef back in the pot, and add the tomato paste with the tomato sauce, oregano, cumin, paprika, black pepper, red pepper, salt, onion powder, and granulated garlic. Stir well.
4. Bring the mixture to a boil, reduce the heat to low and allow it to simmer, uncovered for 1 ½ hours, stirring occasionally. Serve hot, garnished with toppings.

Chicken and Dumplings

This is a favorite classic in the South. Filled with aromatic flavors of thyme, garlic, and heavenly seasonings, this dish will soon become a favorite in your household too. You can whip up this old fashioned Southern recipe any time you're craving some soul-satisfying soup.

Makes 2servings

Ingredients:

- 1 whole chicken
- ½ teaspoon dried thyme
- ½ teaspoon garlic powder
- 1 teaspoon chicken bouillon granules
- 1 cup milk
- 1 teaspoon bacon drippings
- 3 cups self-rising flour
- 1½ teaspoons of salt, separated
- ¾ teaspoon pepper
- ½ tablespoon poultry seasoning
- ⅓ cup shortening
- Water

Directions:

1. Place the chicken in a Dutch oven, and sprinkle with, garlic powder, thyme, ½ teaspoon of salt, ½ teaspoon of pepper. Fill halfway with water and bring it to a boil.
2. Cover with the lid, and reduce the heat to medium-low, allow it to simmer for at least an hour.
3. Remove the chicken to a platter, but reserve the broth.
4. Allow the chicken to cool for 30 minutes, then remove the skin and bone and shred the meat into small pieces.
5. Skim the fat from the broth. Put the shredded chicken back into the pot, and add 1 teaspoon of salt, ¼ teaspoon of pepper, and bouillon granules. Simmer the mixture while preparing the dumplings.
6. In a bowl, combine the flour and poultry seasoning. Cut the shortening and bacon drippings with a pastry blender until crumbly. Stir in the milk until the dough forms a ball. Do not overmix.
7. Turn the dough out onto a lightly floured surface. Roll to ⅛ inch thickness, and cut it into 1-inch pieces.

8. Slowly, drop the dumplings into the simmering broth, stirring it gently. Cover and simmer for 25 minutes.

9. Serve in a large serving dish.

Meat Pie

The Southern styled meat pie is among the most favorite comfort foods for pie lovers everywhere. This recipe is packed with flavor and Serves:a delicious meal. Reach for this great dish if you are looking for an easy, convenient dinner idea.

Makes 2servings

Ingredients:

- 1 pound ground pork
- 1 pound ground beef
- 2 celery stalks, finely diced
- 1 green bell pepper, chopped
- 1 large baking potato, peeled and finely chopped
- 1 bay leaf
- 1 teaspoon dried thyme leaves
- 3 cloves of garlic, minced
- 1 small carrot
- 1 large onion
- 1 cup hot water
- 1 teaspoon Worcestershire sauce
- 2 beef bouillon cubes
- 2 tablespoons chopped fresh parsley
- Salt-free seasoning blend to taste
- Salt and pepper to taste
- 1 egg, separated
- 2 tablespoons of water
- 2 sheets frozen puff pastry
- 2 cups shredded cheddar cheese
- Cooking spray

Directions:

1. Preheat the oven to 350°F, and coat a 9x13 inch dish with cooking spray.
2. Put a large nonstick skillet over medium-high heat and mix the ground pork and beef, cooking until brown and crumbly, about 6-8 minutes. Discard the excess grease.
3. Add the bell pepper, celery, onions, and stir, then cover the pan and reduce the heat to medium.
4. Stir frequently, until the vegetables have softened and the onions are translucent, about 4-6 minutes.
5. Make a well in the center of the skillet; place the garlic on the bottom of the pan for a few seconds, and then blend with the meat.
6. Add the parsley, carrot, bay leaf, thyme, potato, Worcestershire sauce, seasoning blend, and salt and pepper to taste.

7. In a bowl, dissolve the bouillon cubes in hot water then pour it into the meat mixture and mix it well. Bring to a boil then reduce the heat from medium to low. Cover and simmer for 10 to 15 minutes until the carrots have softened.

8. In the prepared baking dish, lay one sheet of puff pastry. Gently push the pastry into the corners of the baking dish. Gently spoon the meat mixture into the crust and spread evenly. Avoid adding liquid to the pie as it will cause it to become soggy. Top the mixture with cheddar cheese.

9. In a small bowl, whisk together the egg yolk and a tablespoon of water.

10. Brush the edges of the bottom of the puff pastry sheet.

11. Lay the second sheet of puff pastry on the top and seal the edges by pressing with a fork.

12. Mix the egg white with remaining tablespoon of water, and brush the top surface of the pastry. Poke holes with a fork to vent the crust.

13. Preheat the oven to 350°F and bake the pie until the pastry has turned golden brown. Keep checking your pie after every 15 minutes to prevent your pie from overburning. Serve hot.

Oyster Stew

This recipe for creamy oyster stew has been passed down from generation to generation of New Orleans families. If you wish to give a simple, refreshing twist to delicious seafood flavor, this oyster stew recipe is the one to go for.

Makes 2servings

Ingredients:

- 1 pint shucked fresh oysters
- ¼ cup butter
- 1 shallot, minced
- 1 clove of garlic, minced
- 2 tablespoons all-purpose flour
- 2 cups warm whole or 2% milk
- 1 cup warm half-and-half cream
- 1 tablespoon hot sauce
- 2 tablespoons sherry
- 1/8 teaspoon celery salt
- ½ teaspoon Worcestershire sauce
- Kosher salt and freshly cracked black pepper
- Fresh lemon juice
- Oyster crackers

Directions:

1. Drain the oysters, reserving the oyster liquor.
2. In a small saucepan, heat the oyster liquor and half-and-half over medium heat, stirring continuously for 3 to 4 minutes, until the mixture starts to steam.
3. Add the oysters, cooking for 4 to 5 minutes until the edges of the oysters start to curl.
4. Remove from the heat. With a slotted spoon, transfer the oysters to a plate and reserve.
5. In a large saucepan, melt the butter, and add garlic and shallot. Cook, stirring occasionally, for 4 minutes until tender.
6. Sprinkle the flour over the mixture and cook, whisking continuously, for 1 to 2 minutes.
7. Slowly add milk, cream, hot sauce, sherry, celery salt, and Worcestershire sauce. Stir until it begins to thicken, then add the oysters.
8. Cook on medium to low heat, stirring occasionally, until it has warmed through.
9. Season the stew with salt and pepper to taste, and serve with a splash of lemon juice and crackers.

Kentucky Hot Browns

In seek of comfort? This famous Southern recipe is sure to become your favorite, topped with roasted turkey and delicious Parmesan cheese. You will find yourself in food heaven!

Makes 2servings

Ingredients:

- 4 thick white bread slices
- 12 ounces sliced roasted turkey
- 2 tomatoes, sliced
- 8 bacon slices, cooked
- 1 cup shredded Parmesan cheese
- Mornay Sauce (recipe follows)

Directions:

1. Preheat broiler and place oven rack on the upper position at about 6 inches from heat source.
2. On a baking dish, place bread slices and broil until golden brown on each side, about 1 minute per side.
3. Arrange bread slices on 4 lightly greased individual baking dishes, and top with turkey slices.
4. Pour warm Mornay sauce over the turkey, and sprinkle each evenly with the Parmesan cheese.
5. Place under the broiler until the cheese is melted and golden, about 2-4 minutes.
6. Top with tomato slices and bacon, and serve.

Gumbo

This heavenly recipe from New Orleans will have you going for second servings and maybe even more. Gumbo is one of the shiniest gems in the crown of Southern cuisine. Simply let all the flavors blend into the meat before you let the good times roll.

Makes 2servings

Ingredients:

- ¼ cup vegetable oil
- 3 large boneless skinless chicken breasts
- 1 pound smoked sausage
- 1 large onion, chopped
- 5 tablespoons butter
- 3 stalks celery, chopped
- 1 green bell pepper, seeded and chopped
- ½ cup all-purpose flour
- ¼ cup Worcestershire sauce
- 5 beef bouillon cubes
- 4 cups hot water
- 8 cloves of garlic, minced
- 4 green onions
- ½ pound shrimp, peeled, cooked and deveined
- 1 can stewed tomatoes (14 ounces)
- ¼ bunch flat-leaf parsley, plus some more for garnish
- 2 cups sliced okra
- Salt and pepper to taste

Directions:

1. Season the chicken with salt and pepper.
2. Heat the oil in a heavy-bottomed Dutch oven over medium-high heat.
3. Cook the chicken until browned on both sides, remove, and set aside.
4. Cook the sausage, stirring until browned, remove, and set aside.
5. Sprinkle flour over the drippings, and add two tablespoons of butter, allowing it to cook over medium heat. Whisk constantly until it begins to brown; this will take about 8-10 minutes.
6. Return the Dutch oven back to low heat, add the remaining 3 tablespoons of butter.
7. Add the garlic, onion, green pepper, okra, and celery and allow it to cook for 10 minutes, stirring often.
8. Next, mix in Worcestershire sauce, ¼ bunch of parsley, salt, and pepper to taste.

9. Dissolve the bouillon cubes in 4 cups of hot water and add it to the pot, together with the chicken and sausage, bring the mixture to a boil. Reduce the heat, allow it to simmer for 45 minutes to an hour.
10. Garnish with parsley, green onions, and shrimp. Serve hot!

Mornay Sauce

- Makes 2servings

Ingredients:

- ½ cup butter
- ⅓ cup all-purpose flour
- 1 ½ cups milk
- ¼ teaspoon salt
- ¼ teaspoon pepper
- ½ cup shredded Parmesan

Directions:

1. Melt butter in a saucepan over medium-high heat.
2. Whisk in flour, and cook for 1 minute, whisking constantly.
3. Add milk and bring it to a boil. Reduce heat to medium-low, and continue cooking until it has thickened, about 3-4 minutes.
4. Whisk in Parmesan cheese, salt, and pepper. Continue stirring until the cheese is melted. Serve immediately.

Fried Catfish

Fried catfish is an epic Southern tradition. This delicious recipe is sure to satisfy. Seasoned, and then fried to perfection, this fish will have you hooked.

Makes 2servings

Ingredients:

- 6 catfish fillets
- 1 quart peanut oil
- 1 cup all-purpose flour
- 1 cup stone-ground cornmeal
- 1 teaspoon seafood seasoning
- ¼ teaspoon ground pepper
- ¼ teaspoon hot paprika
- ½ teaspoon kosher salt
- ¾ cup low-fat buttermilk
- Sliced lemon, for serving

Directions:

1. Heat the peanut oil in a Dutch oven on the stovetop to 350°F.
2. In a shallow dish, whisk together the cornmeal and flour.
3. In a separate bowl, combine the kosher salt, paprika, seafood seasoning, and pepper.
4. Pour the buttermilk into a third shallow dish.
5. Season the catfish on both sides with the spice mixture, and then dip the catfish in the buttermilk, holding it over the pan so that the excess drips off.
6. Dip the catfish in the cornmeal mixture, coating it evenly on both sides.
7. Let the fillets rest on a cooling rack for 5 minutes.
8. Gently lower the fillets, 2 at a time, into the hot oil, and fry until they are golden brown, about 5 to 6 minutes.
9. Gently place the fillets on a wired rack to drain.
10. Repeat until all the fillets are fried, and serve hot with lemon slices.

King Ranch Chicken Casserole

This classic Southern King Ranch Casserole recipe is bursting with the goodness of cheese, peppers, and chicken. It's also a super easy fix to dinner time confusion. More importantly, this recipe is always a hit with the crowd – we bet everyone will love it!

Makes 2servings

Ingredients:

- 2 cups cooked chicken, chopped
- 2 tablespoons vegetable oil
- 1 large onion, chopped
- 1 large green bell pepper, chopped
- ¼ teaspoon black pepper
- ¼ teaspoon salt
- ¼ teaspoon garlic powder
- 1 can cream of mushroom soup (10 ¾ ounce)
- 1 (10-ounce) can diced tomatoes with green chilies
- 12 (6-inch) corn tortillas
- 2 cups cheddar cheese, shredded

Directions:

1. Heat the oil in a large skillet over medium-high heat, and sauté the onions and bell pepper until tender.
2. Stir in the chicken, salt, black pepper, garlic powder, mushroom soup, and tomatoes, and remove from the heat.
3. Lightly grease a 13x9 inch baking dish. Tear in the tortillas into 1-inch pieces and layer ⅓ of the tortillas in the bottom of the baking dish.
4. Top the layer of tortillas with ⅓ of the chicken mixture, then with 2/3 cup cheese. Repeat layers twice.
5. Bake the dish in the oven at 350°F for 30 to 35 minutes.
6. Let the casserole rest for 10 minutes before serving.

Pot Roast

A nice bowl of pot roast is a hit anywhere. Look no further than this superb, extremely tasty, and classic southern pot roast recipe if you have been searching for something to serve at weekend parties or family dinners. This dish is best served with mashed potatoes and roasted green beans.

Makes 2servings

Ingredients:

- 1 boneless bottom round roast (3 to 4 pounds)
- ¼ cup vegetable oil
- 2 yellow onions, peeled and quartered
- 3 cloves garlic, crushed
- 2 cups beef broth
- 2 bay leaves
- 2 fresh thyme sprigs
- 3 carrots, sliced into ½ inch pieces
- 1 cup red wine
- 1 tablespoon tomato paste
- Kosher salt and black pepper to taste
- Fresh parsley leaves, chopped

Directions:

1. Preheat oven to 350°F.
2. Season the roast with both sides with salt and pepper.
3. Heat oil in a Dutch oven over medium-high heat and sear the roast on both sides. Remove the roast from the pot and set aside.
4. Combine the tomato paste, garlic, onions in the pot, and allow the mixture to cook until it has colored.
5. Add the thyme, bay leaves, broth, and wine, and place the roast in the liquid.
6. Bring the mixture to a simmer, then cover and place in the oven.
7. Allow the pot to roast for 1 ½ hours, and then add the carrots. Cook for another hour.
8. Transfer the roast to a cutting board and allow it to rest for 10 to 20 minutes before carving.
9. Skim the fat from the braising liquid, and serve it piping hot over the meat, with freshly chopped parsley.

Chapter 6: Sides

Pickled Green Tomatoes

These crunchy and delicious pickled green tomatoes will go perfectly with ham or grilled chicken. Try this recipe as a perfect relish for any lunch or dinner plate.

Makes 2servings

Ingredients:

- 5 pounds green tomatoes, chopped
- 2 tablespoons pickling salt
- 1 large onion, chopped
- 2 cups cider vinegar
- 1 ½ cups firmly packed brown sugar
- 2 teaspoons celery seed
- 2 teaspoons whole allspice
- 2 teaspoons mustard seeds
- ½ teaspoon whole cloves
- 3 cups water

Directions:

1. Season the tomatoes and onions with pickling salt, and let it stand for 4 to 7 hours.
2. Drain the ingredients and pat dry with paper towels, set aside.
3. In a Dutch oven, combine vinegar and brown sugar, and cook over medium heat. Stir constantly until the brown sugar dissolves.
4. Place the celery seed, allspice, mustard seeds, and whole cloves in a 6 inch square of cheesecloth, and tie it with a string.
5. Add the spice bag, along with the tomatoes, onions, and 3 cups of water to the vinegar mixture.
6. Bring the ingredientsto a boil, stirring constantly. Reduce the heat and allow the mixture to simmer, stirring occasionally, for 25 minutes, until the onions and tomatoes are tender.
7. Remove and discard the spice bag.
8. Pour the hot pickles into mason jars, tap the jars to remove any air bubbles, and cover the jar with the metal lid.
9. Process in boiling water bath for at least 10 minutes.

Summer Squash Casserole

Summer squash casserole is one of the most innovative Southern side dishes of all time. It goes great with turkey or grilled chicken. You will find this side dish an ideal pick for nearly every special occasion, holiday, or get together.

Makes 2servings

Ingredients:

- 2 pounds yellow summer squash
- 1 large onion, chopped
- 7 tablespoons butter, divided
- 1 large clove garlic, chopped
- ½ green bell pepper, chopped
- ½ red bell pepper, chopped
- 4 slices plain white bread, toasted
- 1 jalapeño pepper, seeded and chopped
- 24 round buttery crackers, crumbled in a food processor
- ½ cup heavy whipping cream
- ½ pound sharp cheddar cheese
- 1 teaspoon salt
- 1 teaspoon sugar
- 4 large eggs, beaten
- ¼ teaspoon cayenne pepper

Directions:

1. Heat the oven to 350°F, and grease a 2-quart baking dish with butter.
2. Cut the squash to ½ inch thick slices, and boil in salted water for 10 minutes, until cooked through.
3. Drain the squash, and purée in a food processor.
4. Over medium heat, melt 6 tablespoons of butter, add onion, peppers, and garlic, and cook until the mixture is tender.
5. In the meantime, put the toasts in a food processor and reduce to crumbs.
6. Melt the remaining butter and combine it with the crumbs. Set aside.
7. Combine the squash puree, garlic, crackers, cheese, peppers, and onion in a large bowl, and mix well. Stir in the sugar, cream, egg, and seasonings, and blend.
8. Pour the mixture in a baking dish.
9. Top it with toast crumbs, and bake for 40 minutes until browned.

Fried Okra

Fried okra is a favorite Southern classic! Drenched with batter and fried to perfection, this is something you do not want to miss out on. This perfectly crispy okra will have you and your guests coming back for more.

Makes 2servings

Ingredients:

- 10 pods of okra
- 1 cup cornmeal
- ¼ teaspoon ground pepper
- ½ cup vegetable oil
- ¼ teaspoon salt
- 1 egg
- Kosher salt and white pepper vinegar, for serving

Directions:

1. Beat the egg in a large bowl, and soak the okra in it for 10 minutes.
2. In another, medium-sized bowl, combine salt, pepper, and cornmeal.
3. Heat oil in a large skillet over medium-high heat.
4. Dip the okra in the cornmeal mixture, coating it evenly on all sides.
5. Place okra in the hot oil, reduce the heat to medium-low as the okra starts to turn brown. Stir continuously.
6. Drain on paper towels, and serve with salt and pepper vinegar.

Classic Southern Creamy Coleslaw

Crispy, tangy, and crunchy, there is so much to love about this recipe. In fact, this crunchy version of coleslaw looks bright and tastes exactly how it should.

Makes 2servings

Ingredients:

- 1 head cabbage, finely shredded
- 2 carrots, finely chopped
- 2 tablespoons finely chopped onion
- ⅓ cup white sugar
- ¼ cup buttermilk
- 2 tablespoons lemon juice
- 2 tablespoons distilled white vinegar
- ½ teaspoon salt
- 1/8 teaspoon ground black pepper

Directions:

1. In a large salad bowl, mix carrots, onions, and cabbage.
2. In a separate bowl, whisk sugar, buttermilk, lemon juice, vinegar, and salt and pepper until the mixture is smooth and the sugar has dissolved.
3. Pour the dressing onto the cabbage mixture.
4. Cover the bowl and refrigerate for at least 2 hours.
5. Mix coleslaw again before serving.

Cream Cheese Mashed Potatoes

This creamy recipe for mashed potatoes is all you need to brighten up your weekend meals. You can also prepare this side dish ahead of time and reheat when needed.

Makes 2servings

Ingredients:

- 2 packages of cream cheese (3 ounces each)
- 5 pounds baking potatoes
- 1 container of sour cream (8 ounces)
- 2 teaspoons onion salt
- ½ cup butter or margarine
- ½ cup milk
- Parsley, to garnish
- Cooking spray

Directions:

1. Preheat the oven to 325°F.
2. Peel potatoes and cut them into 1-inch cubes.
3. Bring a large pot of water to a boil, and cook the potatoes for 15 to 20 minutes until tender.
4. Drain the potatoes and place them in a large mixing bowl.
5. Add the cream cheese, sour cream, margarine, milk, and onion salt, and beat all the ingredients at medium speed with an electric mixer until smooth and fluffy.
6. Greased a 3-quart baking dish with cooking spray. Spoon in the potatoes mixture, and bake for 10 minutes until heated through.
7. Garnish with parsley and serve.

Red Potato Salad

This pretty potato salad has a great aroma and flavor, plus it goes well with any menu. Aside from the combination of rich potatoes and mayonnaise, this wholesome potato salad is filling and satisfying. For a twist on the flavors, feel free to add your favorite herbs and spices.

Makes 2servings

Ingredients:

- 6-7 medium-sized red potatoes, scrubbed and cut into pieces
- 1 cup mayonnaise
- ½ tablespoon brown mustard
- ¾ teaspoon white vinegar
- ¾ teaspoon celery salt
- 4 hardboiled eggs, roughly chopped
- 1 to 2 celery stalks, thinly sliced
- ¾ cup onions, sliced
- 4 slices of bacon, cooked and crumbled
- Salt and pepper to taste
- Freshly chopped chives for garnishing

Directions:

1. Put the potato chunks in a medium-sized saucepan and then cover with cold water. Bring to a boil over medium-high heat.
2. After the potatoes have boiled, reduce the heat to medium-low and continue to cook for 8 to 10 minutes until they are tender.
3. Drain the potatoes and then set it aside.
4. In a separate large bowl, combine the mayonnaise, mustard, vinegar, celery salt, eggs, onions, bacon, and celery. Mix all the ingredients well and then finally add the potatoes.
5. Season to taste with salt and pepper.
6. Chill the salad overnight or for at least 2 hours, and garnish with chives before serving.

Macaroni and Cheese

The classic comfort food that everybody loves so much. This is my mom's recipe and she would religiously make it for us every Friday for dinner. So warm and creamy!

Makes 2servings

Ingredients:

- 8 ounces dried elbow macaroni (you can also use whole wheat pasta if desired)
- 1/2 cup bread crumbs
- ¾ cups whole milk
- ¼ cup all-purpose flour
- ¼ cup butter, melted
- 1 cup sharp cheddar cheese + ½ cup for topping, shredded
- 1 cup Monterey jack cheese, shredded
- 1 cup processed cheddar cheese, cut into small cubes
- 1 pinch cayenne pepper
- ½ teaspoon paprika
- Kosher salt and freshly ground pepper
- Butter

Directions:

1. Preheat the oven to 350ºF.
2. Bring a large pot of water to boil, add salt, and cook pasta according to package instructions. Drain the macaroni in a strainer. Rinse under cold running water and drain to stop the cooking process.
3. Toss bread crumbs and melted butter to coat. Set aside
4. Generously butter a baking dish.
5. In a large mixing bowl, add all the ingredientsEXCEPT the bread crumb mixture, and stir to combine. Transfer to the buttered casserole baking dish. Top with the bread crumbs mixture and cheddar cheese.
6. Place baking dish on baking sheet. Bake until bubbling, and cheesy top is golden brown, about 40-45 minutes. Let cool 5 minutes before serving.

Buttermilk Cast Iron Cornbread

Celebrate Southern cuisine with this heavenly recipe for Southern cornbread. You can serve this quintessential southern staple with soups, stews, and salads to wow your guests and family.

Makes 2servings

Ingredients:

- 2 cups buttermilk
- 1 cup cornmeal
- 1 teaspoon baking powder
- ½ teaspoon baking soda
- 1 cup flour, all-purpose
- 2 tablespoons white sugar
- 2 eggs
- 3 tablespoons butter

Directions:

1. Preheat the oven to 375°F.
2. Add the butter to a 10" cast iron skillet.
3. Place in the oven while you make the batter.
4. In a large bowl, whisk together the flour, baking soda, and baking powder.
5. Add the cornmeal, and mix until the ingredients are well blended.
6. In a separate bowl, whisk together the eggs and buttermilk.
7. Add the sugar, and blend until the sugar is dissolved.
8. Remove the cast-iron skillet from the oven, and tilt the skillet until it is completely coated in butter.
9. Pour the remaining butter into the egg mixture.
10. Add the wet ingredients into the dry, and mix until the batter is smooth.
11. Pour the batter into the cast iron skillet, and place in the oven.
12. Bake for 25 to 30 minutes or until the cornbread golden brown and springs back when pressed.
13. Serve warm.

Fried Confetti Corn

This yummy side dish is sure to have you asking for seconds. Simply nestle this dish next to a plate of greens to enjoy a healthy, heartwarming meal.

Makes 2servings

Ingredients:

- 6 cups fresh corn kernels
- 8 bacon slices
- 1 cup sweet onions, diced
- ½ cup green pepper, chopped
- ½ cup red pepper, chopped
- 1 package cream cheese (8 ounces)
- 1 teaspoon sugar
- 1 teaspoon salt
- 1 teaspoon pepper
- ½ cup half and half

Directions:

1. In a large skillet, cook the bacon over medium-high heat for 6 to 8 minutes until crispy.
2. Drain the bacon on paper towels, reserving about 2 tablespoons of drippings in the skillet. Coarsely crumble the bacon.
3. Sauté the corn, bell peppers, and sweet onion over medium-high heat for 6 minutes until tender.
4. Add cream cheese and the half and half, stir the mixture until the cheese melts.
5. Stir in the sugar, salt, and pepper.
6. Transfer to a serving dish, and top with bacon.

Southern-Style Collard Greens

You've read about collard greens, but have you tried them? Because this recipe yields the tastiest greens, you need to look no further if you have a special affection for them. And don't forget to make this recipe an integral part of your traditional Southern feast if you love soulful flavors.

Makes 2servings

Ingredients:

- 2 smoked ham hocks
- 2 sweet onions, finely chopped
- 3 containers of chicken broth (32 ounces each)
- 4 cloves of garlic, finely chopped
- 3 packages of collard greens (1 pound each)
- 2 tablespoons white vinegar
- 1 ½ teaspoons salt
- ¾ teaspoon black pepper
- 2 tablespoons white sugar
- ⅓ cup vinegar

Directions:

1. Combine the garlic, onions, and ham hocks in a stockpot. Add the chicken broth and cook the mixture over medium to low heat until the meat is tender and starts to fall off the bone, about 2 hours.
2. Stir the collard greens, salt, black pepper, sugar, and vinegar into the broth mixture, and cook until the greens have reached the desired texture and tenderness, about 2 hours. Serve hot.

Fresh Corn Cakes

Are you craving something like pancakes? Dive into this appetizing side dish, made with fresh corn, mozzarella cheese, and chives.

Makes 2servings

Ingredients:

- 3 large eggs
- ¾ cup milk
- 1 cup fresh corn kernels
- ¾ cup all-purpose flour
- 3 tablespoons melted butter
- ¾ cup yellow or white cornmeal

- 2 tablespoons chopped fresh chives
- 1 8-ounces package fresh mozzarella cheese, grated
- 1 teaspoon salt
- 1 teaspoon ground pepper
- Chives for serving

Directions:

1. Pulse the corn, eggs, milk, and butter in a food processor 3 to 4 times until the corn is coarsely chopped.
2. Combine the flour, cornmeal, cheese, chives, and salt and pepper in a large bowl. Stir in the corn mixture until the dry ingredients are moistened.
3. Spoon 1/8 cup batter for each cake onto a greased non-stick pan.
4. Cook the cakes for 2 to 3 minutes per side until browned.
5. Garnish with chopped chives and serve.

Feta Stuffed Tomatoes

This is a heavenly side dish bursting with the flavors of fresh herbs and delicious vegetables. The stuffing is healthy and scrumptious.

Makes 2servings

Ingredients:

- 4 large tomatoes
- ¼ cup fine, dry bread crumbs
- 1 tablespoon olive oil
- 4 ounces crumbled feta cheese
- 2 tablespoons green onions, sliced
- 2 tablespoons chopped fresh parsley
- Parsley to garnish

Directions:

1. Preheat the oven to 350°F.
2. Slice tomatoes in half horizontally, scooping out the pulp, and keeping the outside intact.
3. Discard the tomato seeds and roughly chop up the pulp.
4. Combine the feta cheese, pulp, green onions, parsley, and olive oil in a medium-sized bowl.
5. Spoon in the mixture evenly into the tomato shells.
6. Place the tomato shells in a 9x9 inch baking dish.
7. Bake the tomatoes for 15 minutes.
8. Garnish with parsley, and serve.

Okra and Pecan Casserole

The flavor of pecans, combined with okra and crisp breading is a southern side dish you cannot get enough of. If your goal is to bring the delicious combination of pecan and breading into one recipe and stay low on the carb count, this dish is the one you should go for.

Makes 2servings

Ingredients:

- 1 cup pecans
- 1 teaspoon salt
- 1 ½ cup all-purpose baking mix
- ½ teaspoon pepper
- 2 packages of frozen whole okra (10.oz)
- Peanut oil for frying

Directions:

1. In a shallow pan, spread pecans in a single layer
2. Bake at 350°F for 10 minutes, until they are lightly toasted, stirring occasionally.
3. Process pecans, baking mix, salt, and pepper in a food processer until the pecans are finely ground.
4. In a large bowl, toss the okra and the pecan mixture to coat.
5. Pour oil into a Dutch oven, heating it to 350°F.
6. Fry the okra in batches until they are golden brown, 5 to 6 minutes
7. Drain on paper towels and serve.

Chapter 7: Desserts

Mississippi Mud Pie

We've saved the best for last. If you think fussy desserts are no good, you need to think again. Mississippi's favorite mud pie is going to have you wanting seconds...and thirds! This mud pie is going to be every dessert lover's dream.

Makes 2servings

Ingredients:

- ¼ cup sugar
- 1 package cream cheese (8 ounces)
- ¾ cup sugar
- 2 cups graham cracker crumbs
- 3 cups milk
- 1 package instant chocolate pudding mix (3 ½ ounce)
- 1 package instant butterscotch pudding mix (3 ½ ounce)
- 1 container whipped topping

Directions:

1. Combine the graham cracker crumbs with ¼ cup sugar and butter, and press firmly into a large pie plate.
2. Blend the cream cheese and sugar until smooth, and spread on the prepared crust.
3. In a separate bowl, mix the pudding mixes and the milk until well blended and spread this on top of the cream cheese mixture.
4. Top with whipped topping.
5. Chill the pie.

Peach Ice Cream

This 6-ingredient, easy to make dessert will be a hit at home. Don't be surprised if your family and guests keep asking for this amazing chilly treat over and over again.

Makes 2servings

Ingredients:

- 4 cups peeled peaches, diced
- 1 cup sugar
- 1 (14-ounce) can sweetened condensed milk
- 1 (3.75-ounce) package vanilla instant pudding mix
- 1 (12-ounce) can evaporated milk
- 4 cups half and half

Directions:

1. Combine the peaches and sugar in a bowl, and let stand for an hour.
2. Process in a food processor until smooth.
3. In a large bowl, stir together the evaporated milk and pudding mix, then add the peach puree, half and half, and condensed milk
4. Pour this mixture into an ice cream maker, and follow the manufacturer's instructions.

Strawberry Shortcake

It is hard to resist those bright colored gems and this cake is no different. This classic dessert is a big favorite in Southern cuisine. Full of fruity flavors, this dish will be a huge hit with the crowd.

Makes 2servings

Ingredients:

- 2 pounds fresh strawberries, hulled and quartered
- ¾ cup sugar, divided
- ¾ cup cold butter
- 2 large eggs
- 1 cup whipping cream
- ¼ teaspoon almond extract
- 1 container sour cream (8 ounces)
- 1 teaspoon vanilla extract
- 4 teaspoon baking powder
- 2 ¾ cups all-purpose flour
- 2 tablespoons sugar

Directions:

1. Combine the strawberries, ½ cup sugar, and almond extract in a container. Cover with a lid or plastic wrap and allow it to rest for 10 minutes.
2. At medium speed, beat the whipping cream with an electric mixer until foamy.
3. Slowly add 2 tablespoons of sugar, beating until soft peaks start to form. Cover the mixture and keep refrigerated until ready to use.
4. Preheat the oven to 450°F.
5. Combine the flour, remaining ¼ cup sugar, and baking powder in a large bowl. Cut the butter into the flour mixture until crumbly.
6. In another bowl, whisk together sour cream, eggs, and vanilla until well blended, then add to the flour mixture and stir until all the dry ingredients are moistened.
7. Drop dough by lightly greased ⅓ cupfuls onto a lightly greased baking sheet, and bake for 12 to 15 minutes until golden.
8. Cut the shortcakes in half horizontally, and spoon ½ cup of the berry mixture and scoop it on the bottom of the shortcake, top with a tablespoon of whipped cream, cover the top and serve with the remaining whipped cream.

Coconut Layered Cake

Be ready to hit cake heaven with these layers of tropical coconut and whipped cream frosting. This recipe is sure to become a favorite with the crowd at any time of the year.

Makes 2servings

Ingredients:

Cake

- Butter and flour for the baking pans
- 3 cups all-purpose flour
- ½ teaspoon salt
- 2 ⅔ cups sugar
- 1 ½ cups unsalted butter, softened
- 1 cup milk
- 2 teaspoons baking powder
- 1 teaspoon vanilla extract
- 5 large eggs
- ¾ cup sweetened shredded coconut (6 ounces)

Whipped cream frosting

- ¼ cup powdered sugar
- 2 cups whipping cream
- ½ cup coconut flakes
- 1 teaspoon coconut extract
- 1 teaspoon vanilla extract

Topping

- 1 cup sweetened shredded coconut, more if needed

Directions:

1. Preheat the oven to 400°F. Butter and flour 4 (8-inch) round cake pans.
2. Beat the flour, sugar, butter, milk, baking powder, and salt together at medium speed with an electric mixer until well blended.
3. Add the extracts and blend well.
4. Gradually start adding the eggs, one at a time, beating until all the ingredients are blended.
5. Stir in the ¾ cup of shredded coconut, and pour the batter into the 4 prepared cake pans.

6. Bake the cakes for 20 minutes, and then cool on wire racks 10 minutes before removing them from the pans.
7. Reduce the oven temperature to 350°F and bake the 1 cup of shredded coconut in a single layer in a shallow pan, for 10 minutes or until toasted, stirring 2 or 3 times. Set the toasted coconut aside.
8. Beat whipping cream on high speed until foamy, and slowly add the ½ cup of shredded coconut and vanilla extracts, and powdered sugar. continue beating the mixture until soft peaks start to form.
9. When the cakes have cooled completely, spread the whipped cream frosting between the layers.
10. Spread the remaining frosting on the top and sides of the cake, and carefully press the shredded coconut into the frosting.
11. Keep chilled until ready to serve.

Bourbon Pecan Pie

This delectable bourbon dessert is something you will not be able to forget for a long time.

Makes 2servings

Ingredients:

- ½ cup sugar
- ½ cup light corn syrup
- 3 tablespoons butter, melted
- ½ cup brown sugar
- 2 cups pecan halves
- 2 tablespoons bourbon
- 3 eggs, beaten
- 1 (9-inch) deep-dish pie crust

Directions:

1. Preheat the oven to 375°F.
2. In a large bowl, mix the white sugar, brown sugar, and butter. Stir in the eggs, corn syrup and bourbon, and fold in the pecan halves.
3. Pour the filling into the deep dish pie crust.
4. Bake the pie in the preheated oven for 10 minutes, then reduce the heat to 350°F.
5. Continue to bake the pie for 25 minutes until the pie has set.
6. Cool on a cooling rack.

Key Lime Pie

This delectable dessert is especially famous in Key West. You will be surprised how easy it is to make. If you love having something tangy, sweet, and creamy after your meals, this lime pie recipe is for you!

Makes 2servings

Ingredients:

Crust

- ¼ cup firmly packed light brown sugar
- 1 ¼ cups graham cracker crumbs
- ⅓ cup butter, melted

Filling

- 14 oz. can sweetened condensed milk
- ⅔ fresh lime juice
- 2 teaspoons lime zest
- 3 egg yolks

Topping

- 2 egg whites, at room temperature
- 2 tablespoon granulated sugar
- ¼ teaspoon cream of tartar

Directions:

1. Preheat the oven at 350°F and place the oven rack in the middle position.
2. Combine the cracker crumbs, brown sugar, and melted butter in a 9-inch pie plate and press gently to form a crust.
3. Bake for 10 to 15 minutes until it is lightly brown, allow it to cool.
4. Beat the egg yolks until fluffy and light yellow, about 4-5 minutes on high speed. Slowly add the condensed milk, lime juice, and lime zest. Beat until fluffy, about 4-5 more minutes.
5. Pour filling in the cooled graham crust. Set aside.
6. With an electric mixer, beat the egg whites and cream of tartar at high speed until foamy.
7. Gradually add the granulated sugar, 1 tablespoon at a time, and beat the mixture until soft peaks start to appear and the sugar is all dissolved.
8. Spread this meringue over the prepared pie filling.

9. Bake the pie into the oven at 325°F for 25 to 28 minutes.
10. Let cool down and place in the refrigerator 2-3 hours before serving.

Red Velvet Cake

Unsure about what sweet something you should try? This is a delicious dessert you've got to create in your kitchen. Bring the traditional Southern flavors home with this dessert.

Makes 2 servings

Ingredients:

- 2 teaspoons fine salt
- 2 ¾ cups plus 1 tablespoon sifted cake flour
- 2 teaspoons baking powder
- 2 tablespoons red food coloring
- ¼ teaspoon baking soda
- 1 ½ tablespoons water
- 2 sticks unsalted butter, softened, plus some more for greasing pans

- 1 ½ teaspoons vanilla extract
- 2 cups granulated sugar
- ¼ cup unsweetened cocoa powder
- 3 large eggs
- 1 tablespoon finely grated orange zest
- 1 cup whole or low-fat buttermilk

For Icing

- 1 pound sifted powdered sugar (4 cups)
- 1 ½ sticks unsalted butter (¾ cup)

- 1 pound cream cheese
- 2 tablespoons whole milk

Directions:

1. Heat the oven to 350°F, and grease a 9-inch cake pan with butter, then flour. Tap off the excess flour, and set aside.
2. Sift the baking powder, baking soda, flour, and salt twice together, set aside.
3. Whisk the water, cocoa, vanilla, and food coloring in a small bowl until smooth, set aside.
4. In a large bowl, beat the butter on medium speed with an electric mixer until creamy, about 30 seconds. Add the sugar, ¼ cup at a time, beating about 15 minutes, until the mixture becomes fluffy.
5. Gradually add the eggs one at a time, along with the orange zest, beating after each addition. Add the red cocoa mix.
6. On low speed, alternately add the flour mixture and the buttermilk, starting and ending with the flour mixture. Beat the batter using a spatula, 10 to 12 strokes.

7. Pour the cake batter evenly between two cake pans, and bake for 30 minutes, or until a toothpick inserted in the center comes out clean.

8. Remove the cakes from the oven and allow the cakes to rest for 10 minutes before removing from the pans.

9. In the meantime, prepare the icing. In a large bowl, mix all the ingredients at high speed, gradually reduce the speed until light and fluffy.

10. When the cakes are completely cool, place 1 cake on a serving plate. Spread the icing on the top. Place the second cake on top and spread icing on top and sides.

Conclusion

Soul Food Cookbook for Two has more than just tasty and wholesome recipes inside. You'll also find invaluable tips for streamlining your kitchen time, reducing food waste, and enhancing your meals with cooking hacks and simple techniques to add even more flavor to your favorite dishes.

Ditch the refined and processed ingredients and reawaken your taste buds to the vibrant flavors of southern food that will satisfy your hunger. The Soul Food Cookbook for Two makes it easy with over different perfectly portioned recipes with favorite southern comfort food for healthy eating, plus a handy meal plan to make sure you're starting out on the right path.

Lightning Source UK Ltd.
Milton Keynes UK
UKHW032323230821
389362UK00005B/470